Youth

In

Love

Alfonso Valenzuela

This book was
Edited by Bonnie Beres
Translated by Felipe Vielmann
Cover art by Giovani Pleites

Printed in the United States of America by Patterson
Printing, Benton Harbor, Michigan.

ISBN 0-9763167-0-5

Production and distribution:
Living Ministry, Inc.
livingministry.com

This book is dedicated
To my children:

Alan, Veruschka, and Gustavo

for all the loving energy

they bring to our family

and whose genuine friendship and love

mean the world to me.

Table of Contents

Preface

Through all of the different stages of life that a human being goes through, there is no doubt that one of the happiest, most beautiful, interesting, and with the great consequences, is the one known as dating. It might be the one part of the journey of life that is most filled with love, happiness, romanticism, intimacy understanding, companionship, dreams, and many other wonderful moments that give it a special and unique flavor. It is the stage in life which brings about a feeling of wonderful emotions in such a way that you feel as if you are "walking on clouds." It fills life with an immeasurable amount of ecstasy and it elevates and steals the soul away with an intense and pleasurable sentiment of admiration and happiness. It is the theme of the most romantic songs that exist and the greatest inspiration of the tenderest poems. We all have a bit of musician, poets and craziness and during dating these elements, for many unknown until then, make themselves clearly present, in some perhaps more so than others, depending on the intensity of the relationship.

Dating is the precursor to the most intimate relationship that is known between two human beings, that of marriage. It might be the end of the arduous search for the ideal complement. It is the encounter of two beings that aspire to mutual well-being and happiness. The princess and her prince charming come face-to-face, with a love that is more powerful than death itself, with a feeling that overcomes everything and knows no boundaries, with no problems that it cannot excitedly overcome. And although the title of this work is "Youth in Love," we recognize that not only youth but also adults experience this sweet moment in life that makes us feel young again.

Ah, dating. It is beautiful and at the same time difficult and complex. What should be the entrance into a small heaven on this earth, converts itself, for many, into an obscure alley that leads to shame and bitterness. Why is it that marriage goes wrong for some? What is it that makes the difference? The basic difference lies in the fact that, although some have a good dating, others do not. The foundation of a good matrimonial relationship has its beginnings in dating: healthy dating produce healthy marriages. If you begin well you will finish well. Many have problems in their marriage because they had problems while they were dating; that is why those who fail in their dating relationships are destined to fail in their marriage. A marriage does not fix a bad dating relationship; those who shipwreck in their dating are sure candidates for ruined marriages. And because our married life plays such an important role in our life in general, we can see the vital role that dating plays in the life of all people.

The goal of this book is to help all young people in love successfully go through this stage in life, pointing out the important elements that need to be present in their dating in order to assure, as far as possible, the well-being of their marriage.

Why write another book about dating? For starters, this is a theme that always seems to grab the attention of all young people. Also, because the more information there is about this issue, the better it is. Ultimately, I believe that what we are talking about here is very important for all young people and this material, which has been presented in various youth meetings, marriage and family retreats, and counseling sessions, has shown its effectiveness. Many have expressed their desire to have it in a written format in order to review it and share it with others.

After having participated in many question and answer sessions during youth meetings and after many hours spent in conversations with parents of young people and adolescents, I have managed to focus the themes which appear to be of most interest and need for those young people who desire pertinent and fitting information dealing with dating.

The main purpose of this book is to present some ideas that can help every young person to prepare themselves for the enterprise of marriage. Because the majority of young people end up getting married and due to the influence and tremendous impact that marriage has on the life of each person, how important it is to know as much as possible in order to achieve a happy marriage.

The ideas which are presented here have a double intention. First, they are to orient young people about the social and psychological dynamics that intervene in the selection of a mate, to understand how they can know if they are truly in love, the characteristics of good dating, and the probabilities of whether it will fare well in their marriage. The second intention is to help parents and counselors with ideas and materials that might be of use to them as they speak with their children and other young people that are looking for advice on this subject.

In the literature dealing with family life, the subject that researchers are most interested in is in the area of marriage happiness. This is due, without doubt, to the fact that it is an important topic and to the general interest among people to know more about this highly significant subject.

Of course, there are many factors that come into play in the formation of a healthy dating and in the establishment of a good home, therefore, only those elements which are considered to have the most importance will be presented in this book.

I want to manifest my sincere gratitude to all the churches where I have presented seminars about marriage and family and especially to the youth groups for their important questions which have allowed me to focus correctly in the direction of the material that is before you. I would like to express my gratitude to Nibia Mayer and Viviana Calandra for their commentaries and corrections to this manuscript. I am also in gratitude to all my students in the Marriage and Family Class, especially to the pastors from the United States and Colombia for their interesting observations regarding this material. And last, but not the least important, to my beloved girlfriend and wife Jeanine, who has allowed me to personally experience the delights of true love.

Alfonso Valenzuela
Andrews University

Chapter 1

What is Dating?

Michael and Maribel felt a very special attraction for each other almost from the very moment they met. They were both young people that were waking up to that moment in life when both their biological and psychological chronometers were indicating to them that the time had come to find a significant other.

It was the first time that Michael felt this way about a girl. What should he do? What if Maribel rejected him? What would his parents and friends say? The uncertainty burdened him and he had asked himself several times: "why am I looking for problems?" But a power stronger than reason made him become closer to Maribel. After being friends for several months, they became special friends, then they dated exclusively, after which they became engaged, and later they took that important and often dreamed about step towards marriage. Generally, this is the process which young people go through before reaching the altar.

And as I mentioned before, there is no doubt that one of the most beautiful stages in life is that of dating, when everything appears through rose-tinted glasses. One looks upon life with optimism and there are no difficulties that cannot be overcome, there is no obstacle that cannot be overtaken, there is nothing that can bring more pleasure than to be with the one you love. However, it is also a difficult and very critical period that can bring disastrous consequences and results for those involved. Michael and

Maribel very much enjoyed the moments of ecstasy that their dating brought them, but there were several tensions and moments of doubt and uncertainty wondering, What if they took the wrong path? What if they made a mistake that they would regret for the rest of their lives?

In this first part I want us to pay attention to some of the characteristics of dating that are considered to be some of the most important and that stand out, as well as some of the consequences that are the most transcendent. We will especially note the elements that can help in order to have a good dating.

One of the Most Important Steps in Life: Be Careful, Proceed With Caution!

Of the greatest decisions that a human being has to make in his or her life, without doubt one of the most difficult is in relation to marriage. The consequences of such a decision are transcendent and truly affect each individual for the rest of their existence. And of all the stages in life none should be considered with such caution as this one. "If those who are contemplating marriage would not have miserable, unhappy reflections after marriage, they must make it a subject of serious, earnest reflection now" (Ellen G. White, *The Adventist Home, 43*).

A family counselor notes, and correctly so, that it appears as if young people preoccupy themselves more when they are going to purchase a vehicle than when they are looking to get married. When they have to make a decision about any issue, they generally search for advice from people with experience, but when it has to do with marriage they do not want anyone to tell them anything; they consider themselves proficient in the subject and they allow themselves to be led exclusively by their feelings and emotions.

If there is a matter that should be considered carefully, and in the which advice should be sought from experienced persons and of age, it is marriage; if at any time the Bible is needed as a counselor, if there was a time when Divine direction should be sought, it is before giving a step which is to unite two people for the rest of their lives (Ellen G. White, *Messages to Young People*, p. 462).

Better a Dating That Goes its Separate Ways Than a Marriage That Falls Apart

It is not as important if it goes bad and you have to end that relationship in your dating life; but it is important, very important, if it goes bad in your marriage. It is better to end a bad courtship than to proceed into marriage and have to end a relationship after you are married. There is an author who tells us that divorce should happen before marriage, not after. Dating is there so that you can get to know each other to see whether you can make a marriage work. If while you are dating you discover that you do not get along well and that getting married would be a mistake, it is best to end that relationship. The couple can then search for better paths in their lives; but husbands and wives will never find other pathways on which to journey.

It has been estimated that a third of all marriages that fail have shipwrecked before the wedding invitations have ever been printed. Instead of calling them failed marriages they should be known as failed courtships.

It happens many times that couples discover that a marriage between them is not going to succeed, but they feel that they are too far into their relationship, or they have already become engaged and the invitations have already been made and wedding dress has been bought, and they prefer to continue with their plans knowing fully that there are several issues that are already against them, that there are several factors that will not allow them to be completely happy in their marriage. How do you proceed in such a situation? Ending this type of involvement is not easy, especially when so much has been invested in the relationship, but the best possible path is definitely to end it.

It is preferable, without doubt, to end this dating or engagement, rather than to continue and proceed with a wedding:

> "Even if an engagement has been entered into without a full understanding of the character of the one with whom you intend to unite, do not think that the engagement makes it a positive necessity for you to take upon yourself the marriage vow and link yourself for life to one whom you cannot love and respect. Be careful how you enter into conditional engagements; but better, far better, break the engagement before marriage than separate afterward, as many do" (Ellen G. White, *Adventist Home*, 48).

It is better to repent before than after. It is better to hear "she was left at the altar," than to later hear, "Poor thing, the marriage did not work out, what will happen to her and the kids?"

The Purpose of Dating

The time of dating is there precisely for the purpose of getting to know the other person and to discover if it is advisable to marry. And there is nothing or anyone that should obligate a couple to get married when one of the two, or both, determines that it is better to end their relationship and then search somewhere else.

If two people have reached courtship status it is because there are certain factors that favor them, that is to say, there is a certain affinity and attraction. But there are still certain things that they need to find out about each other: their likes, personality, weaknesses, and many other important things.

The partner that fails to see during their dating runs the fatal risk of an adventure of faith that generally ends in disgrace. An author points out that even a happy and confident dating goes on to be a discordant and unhappy marriage. That is why during their dating both partners need to open their eyes wide and then close them once they have gotten married. Unfortunately, in most cases it is the opposite that happens: couples never see any problems until they get married. After the wedding they feel disappointed and frustrated because that was not the person whom they had decided to marry; it is almost is if it is a completely different person that came to the altar. That is why Dr. James Dobson, in his book *Love for a Lifetime,* says that during dating we should open our eyes wide and close them after the wedding. And the truth is that as the saying goes, "love is blind but marriage opens the eyes."

Marriage, the Number One Priority

If this book captured your attention it might be because you already have a partner or because you are looking for someone to date and are seriously thinking of getting married in the not too distant future. And I am almost certain that several of your friends have told you that if you get married you are going to be inducted into the "club of the oppressed" or that you are going to "lose your freedom."

Others have said that "marriage is like a demon," and that "the wedding march is just like any other march: it is played before going into battle," and that "Jesus Christ instituted marriage with the words 'Forgive them for they know not what they do.'" Marriage, however, is the relationship that every young person considers of prime importance.

Despite all the jokes and pranks about marriage, and despite all of the terrible problems that actually attack the family and married life, the number one priority for young people today is the hope of having a good and healthy marriage. *Newsweek* magazine in their Summer/Fall Special Edition of 1990, which was dedicated to young people, mentioned a study that showed that young people chose as their number one priority to have good marriages and a satisfactory family life. And in the same magazine, in May of 1993, we find a study that found that the factor that brings the most happiness is to have good interpersonal relationships, followed by a good marriage and, third, by a religious faith. Cited in this article is psychologist David Myers, who found through his research that the least happy people are those who have a bad marriage, while the happiest people are those that were married to their "best friends." Myers concludes by saying that this not only describes married relationships but also life in general, a life that is full of happiness.

Several authors have pointed out that a happy marriage is one of the most important ingredients for a good life. A great number of people that get divorced will get married again, which indicates that, although the previous experience was bad, they still believe in marriage.

The reason is very obvious. All young people need a special companionship and intimacy that can only be found through marriage. It is a necessity that is so important that human beings do not find peace until this need is satisfied. And the vast majority end up getting married. There is a Brazilian saying that "Men are devils and there isn't a woman who would deny it, but all of them want a devil to take them away."

Despite the painful experience that everyone who gets divorced goes through, marriage continues to be the preferred relationship for the majority of men and women today. This is due, no doubt, to the fact that in our society the marriage relationship is one of the few places where opportunities arise to satisfy the important necessities of intimacy and security. The structure of marriage and the marriage system might change, but the institution of marriage will remain forever.

The Majority Gets Married, Divorced, and Married Again

Statistics in family studies reveal that 96 percent of young people end up getting married sooner or later, and that the majority sooner rather than later. That is to say, many get married before they are ready. It has also been found that the average age at which women get married for the first time is 21.3 years of age and for men it is 23, although it appears that the number of those who wait to get married at an older age is rising considerably.

The factors that make young people wait several years more to get married are varied and complex. One of the most important, no doubt, is to be sure, through different means, to make the correct decision. Although there might be other non-legitimate reasons, if the wait is to assure themselves of a good marriage, those who decide to wait are taking a step which they will never regret.

Unfortunately, it does not go well for all, because out of 96 percent of the people who choose to get married more than half end in divorce. The number of couples that end in divorce is higher than ever, estimated at 53 percent. And although the majority of couples end this way, statistics show that of those that get divorced, 80 percent get married again. They do not give up because they believe in the importance of married and family life. The sad fact is that of those that choose to marry again, two-thirds will get divorced again.

Nobody goes into marriage with the hope that it will go bad or with the desire that it will end in failure. Everyone desires to achieve success and to attain a happy marriage. And if it ends in failure the first and second time, they do not give up and continue to try as many times as necessary with the innate sense of reaching the happiness to which they are entitled.

A very relevant question is, Why is it that marriages go well for some people the first time, while for others it goes bad, even when they continue to try several times over? What important factors intervene in the correct selection of a mate? These questions will occupy our attention in the next chapter.

Chapter 2

Why Marriage Goes Bad for Some People?

As we saw in the last chapter, a little more than half of all marriages that go bad end their relationships in divorce. There is no doubt that whatever endeavor that ended poorly more than 50 percent of the time would not continue producing that product. Marriage, however, is so important and special to human beings that the majority continues in their attempts.

Even the most conservative researchers have clearly indicated that the proportions of divorce cases are exaggerated and that something definitely has to be done about the issue. Otherwise, one of the pillars of society - such as marriage- will succumb, and together with it many other values of supreme importance will perish from our society.

The Base of the Church, the Society, and the Nation

It has been accurately said that family is the foundation of society. As it goes in with the family it will go with society in the nation in general and, as a result, also in the church. If the family structure has problems, then the church will have problems, society will have problems and, as a result so will the nation. And just as family is the foundation of the church, society and, nation, marriage is the base of the family structure. If marriages begin badly we can only expect that the family will go bad as well.

There is a reason why experts say that whatever happens in a marriage will be reflected in family life and as things happen with the family so it will happen to the community. When we speak of marriage, we are dealing with nothing less than the foundational blocks of the entire cultural structure of humanity.

It is of ultimate importance, therefore, to ensure that marriages function positively for the good of our society, of our nation, and of humanity in general. And that is where the heavy responsibility falls upon the men and women that choose to enter into the ranks of this important institution.

The Crisis of Modern Marriages

Marriage, which is the basis of our church, our society and our nation, is nonetheless succumbing under terrible pressures which hound it and today, as never before, it is going through a terrible crisis. The biggest evidence that we have lies in the simple fact that today, as never before, marriages are shipwrecking due to the problems encountered in day-to-day living and the vast majority of those who get married end up smashing themselves upon the terrible and painful rocks of divorce.

Dr. David Mace, who together with his wife has dedicated many years to the study of modern marriages, clearly describes the situation of the marriages of today in his book *Close Companions* with the following words:

"The American family is breaking apart," said Urie Bronfenbrenner from Cornell University, a highly respected family specialist, in an interview that was conducted in "Psychology Today." It is an alarming declaration. There exist, however, many who would agree. The evidence is constantly before us due to the increasingly high rate of divorces; torn apart homes; reports of domestic violence involving women and children; undisciplined youth, perturbed and delinquent; and many other indicators of internal break ups in our homes. We read about it in the newspapers and magazines; we see it and hear about it on the radio and the television; we find it in the social circles in which we move; we even come face to face with it among our friends and family. Whether we see this as the coming about of a disaster that has to happen, or a cultural change, or as an emancipation, something is happening to something that has been considered throughout history as the foundational rock of human society (p. xi).

And we must remember that in each marriage crisis it is not only the couple that suffers but all the members of the family that are affected – directly or indirectly. There are no winners in family fights and conflicts because everyone experiences great pain. And it is definitely true that those who suffer the most are the children.

Main Reasons

What are some of the principle causes of why marriage goes wrong for some? The biggest problem of modern marriages is that those who enter into this relationship do not know exactly what it is that they are doing and they have not learned the most important dynamics and the factors that constitute a happy marriage. These can be multiple and very complex factors, depending on each relationship.

In the following section I will mention those factors which are considered to be the ones that stand out the most.

Lack of Needed Attention

There are people who think more about, study, read, pray, and ask for help on how to purchase a home or a vehicle than they do about the subject of marriage. The opinion of others means a lot to some and affects them greatly on certain subjects, but when it comes to dating and marriage, they are experts on the subject and do not want anyone to tell them anything. They do not pay the proper and necessary attention about something that is so transcendental to their lives. They do not know exactly what it is that they are doing; the consequences that are transcendental when you take this step are unknown to them and therefore they are not properly prepared to take it.

It would be a good thing if there was some sense of instinct involved in this deal, but it has been proven that what is most important is to seek counsel, to be instructed, and to learn about interpersonal relationships between boys and girls to ensure a better courtship and with that a better marriage.

When serious plans are made to take this step, it is important to listen to what others have to say, primarily parents, friends, and people with experience. Studies that have been done about the factors that affect marriage satisfaction should be considered, reading as much as possible on the subject, attending seminars, and participating in courses dealing with dating and marriage. How important it is to learn about the experience of others in order to avoid their problems and enjoy their successes.

High Expectations

There are many people that go into marriage with the highest of expectations. They believe that the romance is supposed to last forever. They want to believe that their honeymoon will last for their whole life. Unfortunately, soon after the wedding the vast majority has no more honey and is left with only the moon. After a short while there is a tremendous emotional shock due to the fact that they expected one result and ended up with something different. When the expectations of our fantasies and dreams come face to face with reality, that's when terrible frustration and desperation enters. It was not what they were waiting for. It was not for this, or because of that, that they got married. They feel betrayed by life. It is very important to talk about what role each will play within the marriage, to know what they expect from each other. That is to say, you have to attempt to put your feet down in reality as soon as possible. In order to achieve this objective, the counsel from professionals, friends and family, can be of great help.

It is very important that the couple spends a lot of time talking about personal expectations that each of them has of the other in regard to marriage. They need to discuss how each feels in regard to such things as chores in the home, work, the process of making decisions, home finances, children, the relationships between themselves and their parents and the rest of their families. Each person needs to know, beyond a shadow of a doubt, what their expectations are and what the expectations of their partner are. They need to talk about it to clear things up as much as possible.

Blaming Destiny

There are some people who are somewhat fatalistic and think that a good marriage and a successful and happy family life are the end result of coincidence or fate, and therefore there is absolutely nothing that can be done in this regard. They believe that if something goes wrong, it was already written and predestined in some way and therefore fate is to blame.

They believe that a good marriage is born that way, that people who have good marriages are lucky. These are the people who say: "They were very lucky, they got to have a good marriage," or: "Poor thing, it went so wrong, what bad luck they had." This type of thinking is far from the truth because, as we will see in a moment, there is not the smallest bit of doubt that a good marriage and a happy family life are not born but, rather, they are made. And this requires constant and coordinated efforts from the married couple-to-be. Marriage, therefore, will become that which the spouses to be wish it to be.

Lack of Commitment

A majority of people consider marriage in a totally light, trivial manner and without the least determination of a serious commitment that is willing to go through all of the difficulties of life.

For this type of people the words, "Till death do us part," have no meaning whatsoever; they lack importance, and this is due to the fact that the last thing on their minds is a lifelong commitment. There are people who purposefully ask that these words not be said in their wedding. This type of liberalism brings about a separation within the marriage the moment the people involved face a significant problem, and all because there is a lack of a duty-bound commitment that concentrates on the marriage relationship as that which is most important and that allows them to see the light at the end of the tunnel, helping them to find an answer to their problems in some way. When marriage is taken lightly and not as a lifelong commitment, divorce is always "the easy way out." And although divorce is the easy way out, it comes with some very difficult consequences.

It is very important to remember that marriage is a very serious subject-an investment and commitment for the rest of our lives. Whoever is not convinced of this truth should never take this step.

The Rushing

One of the reasons why many marriages end up in failure, and perhaps enemy number one of many courtships and marriages, is the rush that many young people, go through for different reasons. As Dr. Ricardo Norton says: "Get married in a rush and you will live a bitter life." And because people do not want to live embittered lives, they end up getting divorced. They rush to get married and then they rush to get divorced.

We find that rushing into marriage is one of the deceits of Satan:

> Satan is constantly busy to hurry inexperienced youth into a marriage alliance. But the less we glory in the marriages which are now taking place, the better.
>
> In consequence of hasty marriages, even among the professed people of God, there are separations, divorces and great confusion in the church (Ellen G. White, *The Adventist Home,* 80).

The general rule is that those who get married quickly, without getting to know each other properly, will end up getting divorced quickly. They do not give each other the proper amount of time to get to know each other during the time that they are dating. Then they get married in a rush and when problems come they don't give each other the proper time to learn how to resolve them and they end up getting divorced. Many people who get divorced would not if they would give themselves more time.

The marriage relationship requires great amounts of time; time to get to know each other before you get married and to make an assured decision and time to get to know each other after you get married in order to learn how to fix the problems of life and therefore achieve a better adjustment. But many people act in such a rush that they do not take the time for premarital counseling and they get divorced so fast that they do not have time to be counseled. Dr. H. Wayne House, in his book *Divorce and Remarriage,* tells us that many divorces are truly unnecessary, because if each of the parties were willing to receive counseling in order to make their relationships work, many of the marriages that end up in divorce could be rescued.

As a result of the aforementioned problem, many decide to get married as a test, or better yet, they decide to live together, which is not truly getting married. The emotional instability and lack of security due to the lack of commitment is evident in these relationships.

Further on we will see more regarding the marriage problem, as well as the sociological and psychological factors that determine happiness in the home, particularly the divine plan for our lives regarding the choosing of a mate.

Before anyone decides to get married, this should be considered seriously and carefully because something that could be true happiness and joy can turn into a terrible disgrace and something utterly bitter. And as we will see later on, everything begins during dating. If something stars off properly, it will end properly. And the people that have serious problems during their dating cannot expect that their marriage will go well.

Before we see the important elements that go into choosing a mate and what constitutes good dating, let us see what some of the reasons are why the vast majority of young people decide to get married.

Chapter 3

Why Young People Get Married?

There is a story that once upon a time there was a very rich man that threw a great party in honor of his daughter who had reached the age of marriage. The most handsome and gallant young men were invited to this special occasion, during which the heiress was to choose her boyfriend from among all of the aspirants and candidates.

After dinner, the father and the future bride invited all of the young men to enter the area where the pool was located. They asked that all of the young men find their places at the opposite end of the pool from where the father and daughter were at and he made the following announcement:

"Ladies and gentlemen," he said in a commanding voice, "we have come together on this special occasion because it is the time when my beloved daughter, heiress of all my wealth, will choose her future husband. This person must be not only attractive, but he needs to be sure of himself and brave enough to face the great problems of life. This man's bravery will be tested on this occasion. The only thing this person needs to do is come across the length of this pool and reach where my daughter is standing."

"That is easy," said all of the young men that were present. But as they approached the edge of the pool they noticed that the water was filled with alligators, crocodiles, and piranhas.

They were all amazed as they looked upon the spectacle in the pool. Who would be brave enough? Who would dare to take on such a risk? Who would think of such a test?

A deep silence hung over all of the people that had gathered, when all of a sudden there was the sound of someone splashing into the water. Swimming faster than the people around could follow and without holding back his emotions, the brave young man came out of the water and went to stand beside the beautiful young woman.

Without a pause people began to yell and in disbelief and happiness. Everyone ran toward the young brave man, hoping to hear the first words out of his mouth after having gone through such an ordeal. The future father-in-law came close and greeted him and asked him what it is that he wants. After a few minutes, the young man caught his breath and said:

"There is only one thing that I want and that is to know who pushed me."

Many young people are "pushed" into marriage in the same way. There are several reasons why young people get married. In his book *Premarital Counseling,* family counselor H. Norman Wright, along with Dr. Grunlan in *Marriage and Family,* mention what happen to be, perhaps, the principal reasons that young people get married. Among them they mention the following:

Pregnancy

Some couples get married because the girl is pregnant. This is what some people call "making him fall" or "entrapment." She gets pregnant in order to make sure that the man will marry her. Many times this is not something that is planned but pregnancy continues to be, and in many cases it is, the end result of premarital sexual intimacy.

Unfortunately many get married "because they have to" or as some say "under the watchful eye of the shotgun." The estimate is that about one-fourth of marriages occur because the bride-to-be is pregnant. Many studies have found that the possibilities of divorce or unhappiness in marriage are very high when the couple gets married because the bride is pregnant.

The destructive feelings of guilt, jealousy, anxiety, spitefulness, and lack of trust are generally present between couples that have to get married for this reason. Therefore, pregnancy is not a reason why two young people should unite their lives in marriage.

Of course, this does not mean that the forgiveness and grace of God cannot be present in a relationship that has been started this way and that the young people that do get married for this reason cannot be happy, but they will need to work much harder in regard to this matter. It would definitely not be best to get married for this reason and therefore it is very important to ensure that you avoid premarital sexual relations at all cost.

Although there are some that advise that couples should get sexually involved prior to getting married in order to know each other better and determine if they truly love each other, it has been proven that this is not really what is in the best interest of those who wish to assure themselves of a good marriage.

Michael Tucker corroborates the results of the previous findings in his study done in 1991: premarital cohabitation does not increase or decrease satisfaction in the marriage.

If getting married due to a pregnancy brings about negative consequences in a marriage, not getting married after having premarital sexual relations also has very negative consequences upon the people that do so.

Unfortunately, in today's day and age there is a very big tendency to have sexual relations before getting married. It is believed that 66 percent of women and 79 percent of men have had sex before their nineteenth birthday. Generally, it happens to girls prior to sixteen and boys before they turn seventeen. More than one million unmarried women become pregnant annually and of those that decide to carry out their pregnancy only 4 percent give their child up for adoption. Of the 96 percent that keep their children, less than half get married.

Although many women believe that by becoming pregnant they will be assured a marriage, if they do not manage to get married the possibilities of getting married to anyone else are very much reduced, because the majority of young men prefer getting married to someone that does not have children. This is as true for men as it is for women.

Spitefulness

Another reason why many young people get married is because of what is known as "spitefulness" or "on the rebound." It is a very common act that some will get married almost immediately after they have broken up from a serious commitment or that their marriages have ended because their spouse has died or they have divorced.

These types of people are the ones that have been very tightly bound to another person and when that person is no longer available, their emotions are transferred to someone else. The problem with this new relationship is that it is based upon the emotions that belonged with the other person with whom the previous commitment was held and not with the new relationship.

Every broken commitment results in a loss and the resulting pain is in direct proportion to the level of intensity of the relationship. It is generally thought that it takes a year to be able to emotionally recover from a loss of this nature. And seeing that a good dating will take approximately six months to three years, every marriage that happens before a year and a half or two years after the loss can be considered as a "rebound relationship."

Rebellion

Rebellion is frequently a motive for many young people to get married. It is also known as the "Romeo and Juliet" syndrome, when young people get married "against wind and tide," although the rest of the world is against it.

Young people rebel primarily against the wishes of their parents and they get married to demonstrate their independence, that they are grown ups and that they can do whatever they wish. And generally the more the parents oppose them, the more attracted the young people feel and the more they want to get married. In some cases, when the parents finally give their consent the young people involved decide that they do not wish to go on with their marriage plans.

The problem with these marriages is that the power that motivates them is opposition or rebellion and not so much the relationship between the two. And when there is a lack of support from the parents, the possibilities of married satisfaction are diminished.

Escape

Many get married because it is the only alternative to get out of home or a relationship where there is any type of abuse, unhappiness, or any other situation that can be considered intolerable. These types of marriages are also based upon another relationship that they wish to escape from and their focus is not necessarily the new relationship, which is of great importance in order to have a happy marriage.

This running away from unsatisfactory relationships generally makes them fall into others that are similar, because the latter relationships are not considered carefully but seen simply as an escape valve. It is very important to find a solution of some kind to the situations that are producing unhappiness and to seriously consider new relationships in which they wish to partake.

Loneliness

Others decide to get married to avoid loneliness. They feel so alone that they decide to get married. Although getting married is a very special relationship of companionship, getting married to not be alone is not enough to maintain a relationship of this magnitude, because marriage brings many demands that come as a consequence of this companionship.

On some occasions, perhaps, every young man or young lady is in need of a good friend, or a close intimate friend, but they are not necessarily looking or in need of a husband or wife.

The Bible tells us that "it is not good for man to be alone" (Gen 2:18). Marriage fills the emptiness that produces loneliness, but getting married solely to not be alone is not enough of a reason, because you can be married and still feel completely alone.

Physical Appearance

Although physical appearance plays a very important part in choosing a mate, this should not be the only element that provides a reason for marriage.

The hypothesis that is known as "matching" indicates that young people generally come together as couples and then get married to others that have the same level of physical attraction as they do. Physical appearance generally is the first impression of the other person; it is the first quality through which we become attracted and, of course, one needs to feel "proud" of the physical appearance of his/her choice, but when this is the only element that leads to marriage, this marriage will not resist the strong storms that will come along which require greater resistance than mere physical appearance.

As we all well know, physical appearance is temporary; as the years go by it begins to disappear. If that is the great and only force that brings together a marriage, then that force will begin to disappear in the same measure that the physical appearance begins to deteriorate. Unless the fountain of youth is found, this is not a valid reason to come together in marriage.

Social Pressure

There are some couples that get married due to strong social pressure that comes from their homes, their church, or from society, and at times from all three combined. The person clearly perceives the indirect messages such as, "What is your problem? Why have you not gotten married?" or, "It is normal to get married, why is it that you have not done it?"

On the other hand, society provides married people with a better social position than people who are not married, in this way exercising a greater influence on many to get married because of social pressure and convenience.

These types of pressures are very strong at times, but they should not be the reason for which a couple decides to get married. On the other hand, these pressures are so powerful, as well, so as to keep a couple married, that is to say, there are many couples that do not separate or get divorced because of the fear of what everyone might say, or think. Although this contributes to the marriage union, it is not necessarily the fountain of happiness for the couple, and it is not the ideal reason that young people should have in order to get married.

Guilt

Many get married because of a high sense of guilt, which is a great motivating strength for those who feel responsible and responsible after having gone through such a long time with another person and having shared physical intimacies.

They have gone so far in their relationship that it becomes very difficult to end it and they wind up getting married because they feel guilty to have reached as far as they have only to take a step back at the last moment. It is better to repent before than after the wedding, because for many the nuptial march will later become a crucial march.

Some young people have asked me, "What is the best way to end a relationship that has lasted for several years?" Whoever thinks about ending a relationship – whether short or long – does so because they are no longer happy in that relationship and if they do not wish to proceed any further it is best to end it. But, what is the best way to do that? There is no easy way out, especially when the other person is still in love. The best thing possible is to be frank and sincere, to explain the situation, to clear up your feelings, and to manifest with sincerity and firmness that you do not wish to continue in this relationship. After all, the other person will do all that is possible so that the relationship will not end and this makes the situation difficult. This is a very hard and painful step, but it is best to end a bad relationship or one that you no longer wish to be in.

Pity

Confusing it for love, many have gotten married due to the fact that they feel pity for a person who has gotten into an accident, that is sick, or finds themselves in some other situation that causes sorrow or shame for that person. This is, obviously, a reason that is very negative for which to take such an important step as marriage.

It is true that some get married to people that cause pity from other people. The important thing is that the person that gets married should not do so for this reason alone. It is very important that what motivates a courtship and future marriage be a reason that is more powerful than shame or pity.

A young lady got married to a man that had two daughters. The little girl's mother had died and the young lady felt sorry for the little girls. The father took interest in this young lady and very soon they were married. Everything was working out until the girls moved to a boarding school. The couple began to have serious problems and ended up separating. That which brought them together was the girls; better said, it was the pity that the wife felt toward the girls. There was no true love between them.

Pity is not a necessary ingredient in the formation of a happy marriage. Whoever is motivated by this feeling should seriously weigh the consequences before taking such an important step as marriage.

Finances

Another heavily weighted reason that young people decide to get married is to assure a certain economic stability as you frequently find in marriage. This happens primarily when one of the two people is economically settled, or because of the convenience that is produced because of the combining of two budgets and the great reduction of expenses that this brings about. But as someone once said, "to get married due to money is the hardest way to earn it."

It is interesting to note that the majority of marriages have problems and arguments due to finances and a high percentage of wives have to work outside of the home. Therefore, there is a need that demands a greater reason than a financial situation to get married and thus have a happy marriage, seeing that when finances are not working, what will hold the marriage together? It is true that finances play a very important role in a marriage, but they are not the main pillar in a happy marriage.

Romance

The dictionary defines the word "romance" as "a sentimental, generous, and fantastic propensity." And during courtship there is, and should be, much feeling and generosity that accompanies this relationship that appears to be fantastic. Everything is beautiful and ideal, because the couple works at doing what is the best possible in order to make the other person comfortable and happy. It is characterized by attention to the small things that please the other person, especially towards the girl. This includes such things as opening or closing the door when she gets into the car or when they go into an establishment, a gift of flowers, chocolates, notes, and pretty words. All of this brings so much happiness to the relationship that it fills it with great proportions of ecstasy and causes life to be seen through rose colored glasses.

Romance plays an important role during courtship and should continue through marriage. But we need to be conscious that it is not all romance in married life. There is not much romanticism in cleaning the house, cooking, washing dirty clothes, changing baby diapers, cutting the lawn and throwing out the trash.

Although many get married for the reasons that were aforementioned, they are all the wrong reasons to get married. And the more of these reasons that are present, the higher the risk of putting together a bad marriage, a marriage that will end in failure. Of course, there are exceptions, but that is exactly what they are, exceptions to the rule.

What then should be the reason to get married? What should be the genuine motive that makes someone want to unite their life in marriage to someone else? I believe that we all have a general idea as to what that reason is and that will be what we look at in the next chapter.

Chapter 4

Love ... and Everything Else

We all know that that only valid reason a couple should get married is because of love. Unless both people are truly in love, the important step of marriage should not be taken. Only true love will help marriages to pass triumphantly through all of the difficulties that will come.

And yet it is difficult to define what love is. It is easier to describe than it is to define. The apostle Paul does it majestically in 1 Corinthians 13. The *New Living Translation* tells us (verses 4 through 7):

> Love is patient
> and kind
> it is not jealous,
> or boastful,
> or proud,
> or rude;
> it does not demand its own way,
> it is not irritable,
> it keeps no record of when it has been wronged,
> it is never glad about injustice,
> it rejoices whenever the truth wins out.
> Love never gives up,
> never loses faith,
> is always hopeful,
> and endures through every circumstance.

An unknown author paraphrased this beautiful "love psalm" in the following way:

I will be patient with you;
I will be kind with you;
I will not have envy;
I will not exalt myself
Nor will I proudly elevate myself over you;
I will not be rude with you;
I will not exploit you to satisfy my egotistical needs
I will not get easily upset with you;
I will not hold a grudge against you;
I will not enjoy myself when you are suffering;
Neither will I listen to gossip about you;
I will always protect you;
I will always trust you;
I will always have hope in you
I will persevere with you;
I will never fail you.

This love is from God, it has divine origin. It is a gift that the Holy Spirit gives us, it comes directly from God. And when we take our time to analyze the characteristics of this love, we start to see that it contains those elements that are ultimately necessary in order to get along in a marriage: patience, the ability to tolerate the weaknesses of the other person; the kindness that helps us to show goodness toward those traits, customs, and mistakes of the other; it is not jealous of the achievements, privileges, or talents of the spouse, on the contrary, you enjoy them; it is not discourteous or selfish, a common characteristic of those that have been married for some years; where there is love there is no anger or rudeness, but comprehension and tenderness, and something that is very important, it does not hold a grudge. It forgives and forgets.

The Fruit of the Holy Spirit

In Galatians 5:22-23 we find the fruit of the Holy Spirit: "love, joy, peace, patience, kindness, goodness, faithfulness, gentleness, and temperance." This fruit contains the beautiful elements of the character and love of Jesus. When we analyze the life of Jesus Christ, we can clearly detect each one of the fruits of the Holy Spirit. That is to say, Jesus is love, joy, peace, patience, kindness, goodness, faithfulness, gentleness, and temperance.

Each person receives this fruit when they receive the Holy Spirit; it is the natural consequence of accepting this gift from God. It is important to note that this does not deal with fruits (plural) but with fruit (singular). It is not a fruit stand where each person chooses what they like the most or what seems best to them; it is one single fruit. This is a fruit that every Christian needs to have in their life because it is the direct result of being in Christ, of having the Holy Spirit.

This fruit grows with the sanctification of the individual, in the same way that fruits grow and ripen. In order to ripen, fruits need to be on the plant, they need to be fed, and they need the rays of the sun. In the same way the fruit (or character) of the Christian needs to mature through the feeding that the Holy Spirit provides and the rays of sun that come from the justice of Jesus Christ.

The Fruit and Interpersonal Relationships

The fruit of the Holy Spirit has everything to do with our life, specifically what we are, our character; and our character definitely affects our relationship with everyone else. During their time with others, the follower of Christ will show this fruit or Christian character. This is what truly distinguishes them and it is hoped that every true Christian will be loving, patient, and benign.

This is truly applicable to the relationship between unmarried and married couples. The character of a person directly affects the relationship with their girlfriend or wife. Let us see how the fruit of the Spirit is applicable to courtship.

The Fruit of the Holy Spirit and Dating

If the fruit of the Holy Spirit directly affects our interpersonal relationships and if it is hoped that we will demonstrate that same spirit with everyone that surrounds us, without a doubt whatsoever this is applicable also to the relationship of courtship. Every boyfriend hopes that his girlfriend will be a person that can show in their life what it means to be a true Christian. Every girlfriend wishes that her boyfriend will be a loving person, full of joy, peaceful, and patient.

Let us look at this more closely. Let us note how each one of these characteristics of the fruit of the Spirit has its application in relationship to courtship.

Love

Dr. Peñalosa, in his book *Mini-talks for Couples*, reminds us that love is the favorite verb for couples. They know it in all its tenses: I loved you, I love you, I will love you. They know it in its singular and plural form; in active and passive voice. In a couple's grammar there is no other word that is as sweet as the verb love. It encompasses all of the words of the dictionary and saying it continually does not allow itself to ever be repeated. Love is the first aspect of the fruit of the Holy Spirit. The love that is described in the book of Galatians is "agape" love. This is the type of love that implies respect and is based on principles, not only physical attraction. This is the love of God and the type of love that is most pure in the highest sense of the word. It is an unconditional love that has a high sense of commitment.

When one looks upon a woman and exclaims "Wow" we are not in agape love. That is, it lacks respect because it treats the other person as an object or an animal that one wishes to utilize, an appreciation that is completely based upon a material level.

We saw how true love is described in 1 Corinthians 13, a love that comes from God. And this type of love is the only thing that will keep a couple together until the end, granting them the ability to confront the problems of family life.

Of the nine aspects of the fruit of the Spirit, the first that is mentioned is love and this is due, without doubt, to the preeminence that love has on interpersonal relationships. I would like to suggest that the following aspects of the fruit are centered and intimately bound to love. That is to say, if there is love, there will be joy, peace, patience, kindness, goodness, faithfulness, gentleness, and temperance. In the same way, where these parts of the fruit are present, there will be true love. As Dr. Barnhouse says:

> Joy is love that is sung,
> Peace is rested love,
> Patience is supported love
> Kindness is the touch of love,
> Goodness is the character of love
> Faithfulness is the habit of love,
> Gentleness is love forgetting itself about itself,
> Temperance is love taking the reigns.

Joy

The next characteristic of a good relationship is joy, the joy of being with the other person. People in love enjoy being in the company of the person they love. They always want to be together. They are each others best friends and they find joy in helping each other and helping each other excel, knowing that this pleases God. There is no true joy when things are done that do not please God.

When it is thought that the behavior between the couple is not pleasing to God, that it is not in agreement with the high moral principles that should govern the life and conduct of every young person, how important it is to change that conduct.

Whoever does not feel joy while being with their boyfriend or girlfriend, it is definitely because something is wrong in that relationship and something has to be done about it. Whoever does not feel pleasure, joyfulness, and happiness while with their boyfriend or girlfriend, whoever does not delight themselves in knowing that everyone else meets and gets to know their boyfriend or girlfriend, whoever is ashamed of him or her, we doubt that there is true love in this relationship.

Peace

First of all, peace has to do with personal peace with God. If there is no peace with God, there cannot be any peace with anyone else, not with a boyfriend or a girlfriend. This peace is achieved when one receives the justification that God grants us through Jesus Christ (Romans 5:1).

Peace can also be applied to the absence of confusion. Peace takes away confusion. If there is confusion in regard to the relationship, then it is important to seriously consider what is happening. Whoever has no peace because they are confused or completely unsure of their courtship has a very powerful reason to detect the probable lack of true love.

If the dating relationship produces friction with everyone around you to the point that it takes away peace with friends, especially with parents, one needs to be very careful, because love should not take peace from anyone, nor does it get people into fights. Love is not exclusivist. It does not eliminate family and friends from the scene; least of all does it turn people into enemies.

This part of the fruit of the Spirit also has to do with fights within the courtship. Where there is peace there are no fights. If there are many fights during the courtship, what hope can there be for the marriage? Bad courtships produce bad marriages. And marriage does not change anyone. If there is hitting and violent streaks during courtship, they are considerably increased in marriage. Many have tricked themselves thinking "Everything will change when we get married." People that do not have peace during dating, will have serious war in their marriage. Talking about married life, the apostle Paul tells us that "God has called us to peace" (1 Corinthians 7:15).

Where there is true love, peace reigns with God, with friends, and with family members (especially parents) and there is harmony for the couple.

Patience

First of all, we must have patience and await the correct person. Many do not love the correct person; what they want is a person-end of story!

As with everything in this life, love has its season and dating has its time. Dating that begin in the spring of life is premature dating. Whoever does not wait for the correct time and person sows a bitter life due to their impatience. There is a time for all and the time period for a courtship also has its times.

Based on what I will present next, I am convinced that there is no time to establish a serious relationship before turning 18 years of age. One needs to be patient and wait. Hastening is contrary to patience. Whoever hastens to become a couple, hastens to become engaged, and then rushes into getting married are the people that later rush to get divorced. Patience also helps us to not quickly become angry with the other person, to not judge before we should, to be on the same page and rhythm as the other person. Without doubt, the courtship relationship and marriage require great portions of patience.

Kindness

Kindness has to do with not demanding attention from your boyfriend or girlfriend. There are those who want to be the complete center of attention for their significant other, not wanting any competition from other friends, and at times not even from family or parents.

A person that is kind is not rude or cruel, but is considerate, looking for the good. It is important to always consider the needs of the other person, to put themselves in their place, to seek first their good rather than one's own.

Goodness

Goodness must reign in every relationship if it is your wish to continue in that relationship. It should be obvious that no one wants to have bad friends and even less to have bad boyfriends or girlfriends because, after all, who wants to get married to that kind of person?

A good boyfriend is a kind and good person that looks after the reputation and overall well-being of his girlfriend. If for any reason the relationship does end, there is no resentment or guilty feelings.

Faithfulness

What is a dating of faith? A dating of faith means not getting involved in a relationship with unbelievers, with people that do not have the faith of Jesus. This is in accordance with 2 Corinthians 6 and with different scientific studies done on this issue that have demonstrated that marriages between people who have different religious beliefs report unhappiness in their marriages.

If the wish is that true love reign in your relationship, the love that comes from God, the couple will not proceed against the divine counsels as established in the word of God. Ellen G. White counsels: "My sister, unless you would have a home where the shadows are never lifted, do not unite yourself with one who is an enemy of God." (The *Adventist Home*, 67).

What about the "missionary dating"? That is to say, to go into a relationship in order to win the other person to Christ. Although it can be a very effective method to bring other young people to the church, one has to proceed with much caution so that the other person does not end up taking you out of the church. And if the person feels that your intentions were nothing more than "missionary" in intentions, they can feel deceived and disappointed. Although the problem does not come from dating unbelievers, but in marrying them, the young Christian will always strive to behave with the dignity of his or her Christian faith and will not go on in their relationship until they are sure that their significant other has genuinely accepted Jesus. Because of this, it might prove best to ask someone else to work with their significant other.

We could also relate a dating of faith with the faithfulness that needs to exist between couples. The couple has to be faithful to each other. Infidelity during courtship is a strong indicator of the possible and almost assured infidelity during marriage. Whoever is unfaithful during dating tends to be unfaithful during marriage. If a young man tends to hang out with other females or if a girl has several boyfriends, or those who have a girlfriend but like to flirt with other girls, could be showing serious indications of a false foundation in the relationship. The couple needs to proceed with extreme caution in this case before taking the step towards the altar.

Faith also has to do with the spiritual growth of the couple. Both need to ensure their individual spiritual growth. They need to encourage each other to study the Bible, attend church, and participate in community outreach. Growing together spiritually will strengthen their relationship.

Gentleness

What is gentleness? One author tells us that gentleness has everything to do with balance. We need to be balanced in our relationship during dating. Three hours of kissing and hugging and ten minutes of communication is definitely an imbalance.

Gentleness also has to do with docility. A person that is gentle and docile accepts criticism constructively and is willing to change their way of life and act in order to strengthen their relationship. They do not become full of anger and spitefulness when someone tells them that they are doing something wrong or that it is possible that this person or that one is not the best partner for them. They are willing to change for the best; they accept advice, and follow the indications of the people around them who have more experience.

Temperance

Temperance is the last aspect of the fruit of the Spirit. Temperance is very important in relationships of young people when they are dating. Temperance has everything to do with self control.

It is so important in dating to insure that one has self control. Do not do anything that can injure the feelings of the other person.

If one of them, particularly the man, wants to go beyond what is correct because he has lost his self control, the woman can help him to control himself by making him see that not everything is allowed while they are dating. Later, he will respect her all the more. If he does not respect her later, she needs to end that relationship because he is not worth it.

The young person that says "I cannot control myself when I am with her, I love her too much," is not truly in love, but in heat, full of passion and infatuation.

We should not be slaves to our glands or hormones. With God's help we can control ourselves.

In our dating, just as in everything else we do, we need to always conduct ourselves as if Christ was present. And He is.

Love and everything else that the Holy Spirit gives us needs to be present throughout our whole courting relationship. If we do not have it, we need to ask for it from God. He wishes the best for us.

God loves us. And God's love demonstrates itself through our parents. They want the best for us. Let us pay attention to their advice. And

"If you are blessed with God-fearing parents, seek counsel of them. Open to them your hopes and plans; learn the lessons which their life experience have taught. If children would be more familiar with their parents, if they would confide in them and unburden to them their joys and sorrows, they would save themselves many a future headache." (Ellen G. White, *The Adventist Home*, 73).

God gives us love so that we can have complete happiness. The devil has something that is similar that produces ruin for all who possess it. It looks very much like love. It is known as infatuation or passion. Infatuation will be what we look at in the next chapter.

Chapter 5

Love or Infatuation?

Alejandro and Jennifer began their relationship when they were in high school. As their dating grew they would spend more time together. The time came when they did not feel well when they were not together. They would lose their appetite. Their dating could be described as "very intense." With all assurance, people could say that their life had three rose colored coats. There were some details that made them doubt their happiness together, but they felt that there was not an obstacle that they could not overcome.

Their intensity took them to very intimate physical demonstrations of their love that escalated little by little until they became sexual relations. The moment came when they could not live without each other. They would have gotten married immediately but they were only 16 years old. With all of their sincerity they had promised each other eternal love and therefore they would patiently wait until Alejandro could find a job. Several months later they reconfirmed the terrible news that Jennifer was pregnant. They felt that the world was falling down on top of them. The pain and the shame that they brought upon their parents was something indescribable and very difficult to bear. And so, in a few weeks, they had to get married.

Everything appeared to be perfectly fine during the first weeks, but about three months into their marriage they began to have serious difficulties. After a year of constant fights and terrible problems, the day came when they ended up separating and a few months later they got divorced.

What had happened to that intense love that Alejandro and Jennifer felt for each other? What happened to that feeling that appeared to be as strong as death itself and that gave them the assurance of overcoming every obstacle that came their way? Evidently it ended several weeks after the wedding. Alejandro especially began to lose interest in Jennifer. He disliked the fact that he had to quit school for her and that he had to start working at a gas station earning minimum wage. They both felt terribly disappointed and deceived. Alejandro began to be violent and came to the point that he hit her. One day, after a very bad fight, Jennifer went home to her parents and never came back. Here is another example of a marriage torn apart by the trap of infatuation.

Something that has caused the ruin of many marriages is the confusion of many couples between what is true love and what is infatuation. They are so alike that at times it is almost impossible to distinguish between them, especially at the beginning of a couple's relationship, and it is because of this that it is very important to give the relationship sufficient time. As time passes, the difference between love and infatuation becomes more evident.

A History of Infatuation:
The Story of Amnon and Tamar

The Bible presents the story of a young man who believed he was crazily in love when what he was only truly infatuated. This young man's name was Amnon. He was no one less than the son of the great King David. One of the biggest problems that Amnon had was his family.

Amnon came from a divided home because his father was involved with several women. And the fact that he was involved with several women brought him terrible consequences. One of them was the one of his son, Amnon.

Tamar was a very beautiful girl, sister of Absalom, and they were both David's children also. Tamar, then, was Amnon's half sister. Of course, Absalom loved his sister Tamar very much. Absalom had one little daughter of whom it is said that she was very beautiful and in remembrance and fondness of his beloved sister, Absalom named his only daughter Tamar.

This of course meant that Amnon and Tamar were half-siblings. And everything appeared to be going well until the moment that Amnon believed that he had fallen in love with Tamar (see 2 Samuel 13:1, 4). We are told that he was so intensely "in love" that he distressed himself until he made himself sick (13:2).

There was no lack of people that gave him bad advice (unfortunately another family member) and Amnon followed that advice and devised a terrible plan to "satiate his love" (13:3-10). He feigned an illness and he asked his father to send Tamar so that she could look after him. Without knowing anything about it, Tamar accepted her father's request and went to prepare food a meal for Amnon. When Tamar brought the food, Amnon took her by force and abused her (13:11).

No matter how much she begged, Amnon would not listen. And he did not hear her because passion does not understand reasoning and it does not hear what anyone else is saying (13:12-14).

Once Amnon satisfied the demands of his "love" something very interesting happened. Once Amnon violated his half-sister, he hated her with a tremendous hate. He did not even want to see her. He came to hate her much more than what he "loved" her (13:15-17).

Was that true love? Amnon believed that he had fallen in love with Tamar, but in reality he had become impassioned with her, he had become infatuated.

Differences between Love and Passion

There is a difference between passion and love. There are young people that believe they are in love, when in reality they are impassioned. This passion is temporary, and is primarily based on the physical. Love is lasting and is based on principles and not mere feelings. Love is benign and long suffering; an impassioned person looks only to their own benefit, it is selfish and looks for its own convenience.

Young people that love each other attempt to spend time in conversation and truly get to know each other. Young people that are impassioned only want to spend their time wrestling and grabbing and touching even that which they should not.

True love waits until marriage. Passion frequently falls into fornication and adultery. Passion ends when the carnal necessities are satisfied and in its place hate and jealousy are born. There is nothing worse than getting married when there is not true love but rather passion in a dating relationship.

Something that has caused the ruin of many marriages is the confusion of many couples between what love is and what infatuation is. They get married in the rush of passion and when the reality of married life arrives, they do not know each other, they come to hate each other, as happened with Amnon. How unfortunate it is to get married when one is infatuated. The problem becomes worse because it is almost impossible to distinguish them, especially at the beginning of the relationship.

Dr. Grunlan in his book *Marriage and Family* has compiled a list of the principal differences between what love is and what infatuation is:

1. Infatuation is born at first sight and conquers all. Love is developed little by little and becomes deeper as real expectations are shared.

2. Infatuation demands exclusive attention and devotion and is jealous of others. Love is based on self acceptance and is shared with others.

3. Infatuation is characterized by exploitation and the direct need for gratification. Love looks to help and fortify the beloved person without looking for reward.

4. Infatuation is based on physical attraction and sexual gratification; sex dominates. Love includes sexuality without excluding the other areas of life.

5. Infatuation is egocentric. It seeks change in the other person. Love finds its center in the relationship. It looks for the growth of both people towards things that are good.

6. Infatuation is pure romanticism. It does not face or fear reality. Love has romanticism but seriously considers reality.

7. Infatuation is irresponsible and fails to consider future consequences. Love is responsible and accepts consequences.

Unmasking Infatuation

To be infatuated means to be "dummied." An impassioned person goes into a surreal and irrational trance from which it is difficult to come out, especially at the beginning, and that is why it is very important to give relationships plenty of time. As time goes by the difference becomes more obvious, couples discover whether what they feel is true love or pure passion. Passion cannot bear the passing of time.

What is interesting is that while people that are impassioned do not see their situation, everyone else does. But there are many who do not say anything because the couple becomes offended or they do not heed the advice that they are given.

Whoever wishes to have a good courtship will give plenty of time to their relationship and they will be very attentive to what everyone around them says about them, especially their parents.

How do I know if I am truly in love? We have seen that the answer is not as simple as it appears; however, certain characteristics of love can help answer the grand question.

Every couple should seriously analyze their situation and decipher, so that there are no doubts left, the nature and purpose of their relationship. I invite you to answer the following questions that are accompanied by pertinent commentary that can help to define the path of your relationship and determine if what unites your courtship is true love:

Are we mature enough for a serious dating and marriage in the near future?

True love requires maturity and this maturity does not come until late in adolescence and the beginning of young adulthood, especially after 20 years of age. A girl that is 13 or a boy that is 14 would do best not to ask whether he/she is truly in love, the truth is that what moves them is not love. Although there is a type of "school sweetheart love," "summer love," or "puppy love," that every young person experiences at a very early age, this love is passing and immature and not the love required for marriage.

A mature person acts with seriousness, responsibility, a high sense of commitment and consideration, pays attention to the advice of others, and behaves as a lady or gentleman should.

Is there too much selfishness in our courtship? Do we seek the good and personal satisfaction?

Love is not selfish; it concentrates on "us" and not on "me." The success, the well-being, and the respect of the other person is more important than one's own well-being. The other person's happiness is sought after and also that of others, even if that requires a certain personal sacrifice.

Do we feel completely happy and satisfied with our courtship?

Love brings happiness and satisfaction. Happiness comes from being with the person that pleases one and because the couple is in agreement on the things that are important in life for both of them. And satisfaction because they have found each other and their energies are concentrated in growing together and planning for the future.

Do we have realistic expectations? Do I know the imperfections of my boyfriend or girlfriend? Am I willing to bear these imperfections without allowing them to bother me to the point that I will not enjoy our relationship?

Love is realistic. It sees the imperfections, weaknesses, and faults of its companion, which must be within the limits of what is acceptable. It is important to know those faults and imperfections and seriously decide if one is willing to accept them or not. It is during dating that this decision must be made and to agree with that decision during marriage. It must be remembered that marriage does not change anyone. On the contrary, many times the faults and weaknesses are seen much more and are endured much less than during dating. It is very important to come to satisfactory terms with the weaknesses that are found in the boyfriend or girlfriend or one should definitely not proceed with marriage.

Do I feel proud of my boyfriend or girlfriend?

The person in love feels proud of their companion. They want everyone to know them, so they know his abilities, plans, ideals, ambitions. If he or she feels bad about being with their significant other or are ashamed of introducing them to others, it might be an indication of lack of love.

Do we share the good things of life and do we enjoy participating in activities that make life enjoyable in a healthy manner and that fortifies our relationship?

Love brings the desire to share together the good things of life, such as the reading of a good book, taking trips through nature, in truth, to participate in healthy activities that make life happy and fortify the relationship.

Do we agree in the moral and religious values that are to govern our relationship?

The people that are truly in love come to a mutual agreement about the moral and religious values that are to rule their lives and relationship. They are not rebels against the general moral principles but rather they look to accommodate themselves to those principles knowing that they can have a great influence on the harmonious growth of their relationship.

Do I believe that my boyfriend or girlfriend is my best friend?

Companionship is of great importance for people in love. Being together brings a great satisfaction without the need to have to do exciting things. To be companions means being the best of friends, seeking the best and protection for each other.

Do we fight a lot in our dating?

Is it possible to have a courtship without any fights? If you are truly in love, will there be problems? Each head is a world, with different ways of seeing things. It is very unlikely that when two people enter into a relationship they will be in agreement over everything. Whoever looks for a perfect relationship will have a very difficult time finding it because it is difficult to find a perfect person. In every relationship there will be differences, and at times fights. You should not fear the occasional argument. What's more, it could be that they are healthy in order to discover how it is that you will resolve your differences. As someone has said, "The important things are not the differences, difficulties or arguments, but rather how they are resolved." The grave problem is when there are a lot of arguments between couples, because if there are difficulties in getting along while you are dating there will be even more difficulties during marriage.

Does our dating bear the test of time?

If any doubts exist about the love that is felt, time is the decisive factor. You cannot be sure of the love that you feel for each other unless you allow plenty of time to go by in order to go through a variety of circumstances. It is possible to be good, attentive, and loving for a couple of weeks, but several months and years will uncover what a person truly is.

It is of vital importance, therefore, to be 100 percent sure that what exists in the relationship of your courtship is true love or some false version of the same. It is of supreme importance that both be sufficiently sure and one thing that will help on this issue is the test of time. As time goes by, passion or infatuation will be unmasked and will disappear because the nature of passion is temporary, while true love is long lasting.

The Importance of the Test of Time

I believe that we have dwelt sufficiently on the importance of waiting and giving the relationship plenty of time. To illustrate the transcendence of this factor, let us take the case of Jorge and Juanita.

Jorge is an 18-year-old young man that recently noticed the beauty of Juanita and felt greatly attracted to her. He had never felt an attraction such as this for any other female. His parents and siblings began to notice something strange. All of a sudden, Jorge began to iron his clothes for himself, he didn't want to wear wrinkled clothes, and he began to ask his sisters about different color combinations. Like never before he wanted to get to church early, and he even carried his Bible and Sabbath School lesson. But his change at home was not comparable to his change at church, especially before Juanita; he was courteous, kind, respectful, a complete gentleman. He appeared to be a completely different Jorge!

Juanita, on her part, also felt the arrow from Cupid's bow. Her parents also noticed her strong interest in arriving at church on time, her interest in getting ready and looking good, of even learning her Bible texts.

Jorge and Juanita were walking on clouds and everyone around them felt the breeze and honey that came off of them. However, something very strange happened. It appeared that as if by some act of magic the courtesy and gentlemanly behavior that Jorge had would disappear whenever he was not near Juanita, which became the object of taunts from his sisters. And Juanita was not as much of a Christian in her home as when she was near Jorge.

What was happening? It is something very simple through which every young person goes when they are fixing their eyes upon someone of the opposite sex. This is something that happens to every young person that enters the "hunting" season.

There two very important things in the life of Jorge and Juanita. Jorge and Juanita behave themselves at home with their true colors (inattentive, showing lack of obligation, and rudeness). But when they are together, they cover themselves with things that they are not (friendly, loving, and attentive) in order to attract the other person, because if the other person saw them as they truly are, they would not be attracted in the least.

The next diagram presents a black center as what Jorge and Juanita truly are and the circle around that represents what they present or want to be and what they know the other person likes.

Jorge and Juanita know that they have to behave themselves in a different way when they are together. If Jorge behaves as he truly is, it will not be something that Juanita likes.

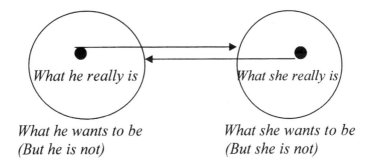

What he wants to be   What she wants to be
(But he is not)   (But she is not)

The interesting part of this all is that Juanita is attracted to Jorge by what he is not, and Jorge is crazily in love because he found the ideal woman, which Juanita is not. The real Jorge is attracted by the ideal Juanita, and the real Juanita is attracted by the ideal Jorge.

Only as time goes by will Juanita begin to discover, little by little, the true Jorge. Time spent in conversation, much conversation, makes it possible for the ideal atmosphere to disappear and for their true selves to be manifest.

Whoever gets married to the ideal, without completely knowing what their boyfriend or girlfriend is in reality, are the ones that a short time after the wedding, many even during the honeymoon, say: "This is not the person I married," "My boyfriend was not like this," "It appears that they changed him on me," "I wish someone had told me who they truly were." Others affirm that from the honeymoon everything began to go wrong in their marriage. They did not get married to the person that they thought they were marrying. And when they "discover" the "real" spouse many decide right then and there to end the relationship or to move forward with an unhappy relationship. But because we are never going to get to know our significant other or spouse in a complete manner, and each time, as time goes by, we discover new aspects of their character, it is important that we seek to adjust ourselves in the best way possible in order to do everything so that the relationship, especially the married relationship, will function well. It is during dating when one can decide not to continue the relationship. That is what dating is for. But once the commitment has been sealed at the altar, one should not retreat. That is why making the correct decision is so important. Time spent in conversation, the advice of friends and family, and the direction of God are the guides that we should learn to appreciate.

We cannot emphasize enough how important it is for couples to truly get to know each other for what they are, their likes, motives, values, and aspirations, and for this great quantities of time are needed. It is with the passing of time that trust is won and that people begin to "lower their guards" and what one truly is begins to manifest itself. Only then is it that the couple can make a wise decision to continue or terminate a relationship, because it is then that one has a good idea of who the other person truly is.

Chapter 6

To Whom Do Young People Get Married?

A little boy told his little friend: "When I grow up I am going to get married to a woman." "Well of course," replied his friend, "who have you ever seen that gets married to a man?" Without missing a beat the little boy answered, "My mom."

Who do young people get married to? Well of course men with women and women with men (in most cases). But what factors intervene in the choosing of a mate? What internal or external forces operate in each young person when we are dealing with the choice of their significant other?

In this chapter we will consider the different factors that intervene in the process that the majority of young people follow in order to select a boyfriend or girlfriend and we will also note some of the important theories that exist on this subject.

Arranged Marriages

Although arranged marriages are not a part of our tradition in Western culture, in many places the parents are the ones that select the mate for their children; they are the ones that decide, at times with much anticipation, who it is that their children are to marry.

These types of marriage arrangements date back to biblical time. We have, for example, the case of Abraham, who arranged the choice of a mate for his son Isaac.

This type of choice begins at a time when the young people are still very small and many do not see their fiancée until moments before the wedding.

In some places of Africa, India, and China, this is still common practice. And what is interesting is that the divorce rates are very low. In a meeting with couples whose marriages had been arranged, it was asked of one of them how they could be happy with someone that they had not chosen. One of them answered, "It appears that our parents are truly preoccupied about our happiness and they do a good job. What I cannot explain to myself is how it is that we who do not choose our mate do not end up getting divorced and you who choose and get married because you cannot live another day without being apart, after a year end up divorced."

The advantage of arranged marriages is that the young person does not have to preoccupy him or herself with the process of choice. Their parents do it happily and with much anticipation. But, knowing that arranged marriages are not a common practice in our culture, the majority of young people have to go through the sometimes worrisome process of choosing who it is that they are to form a home with.

There have been different theories that have been formulated and ideas dealing with how to choose a mate. Let us look at some of the most important.

Opposites Attract

This theory is based on the idea that young people are attracted by people that are different than themselves. It is the process of choice, conscious or unconscious, that procures a balance in the couple. Although generally "opposites do not attract but rather attack themselves," there are certain factors of personality that influence persons to be attracted to people that are total opposites.

There are cases, for example, of some dominant people that tend to get married to people that are submissive and others that are very protective who attempt to find people that desire protection. This can be due to the unconscious desire to look for someone that complements the personal desires and needs that they feel they are missing.

There are couples with very different characteristics that settle themselves perfectly, developing a very good relationship. It is of great importance that the couple discovers and recognizes what the principal differences are between them so that there are no surprises. Then they will need to discover if they can develop a relationship that is satisfactory for both of them. Of course, it is very important to do this during dating and to know at that point if the relationship is to function or not. Whoever gets married without doing so, discover later that it is too late and they end up disappointed or separated.

Likes Attract

This theory is opposite to the previous one. Several studies have indicated that the endogamic factors or similar backgrounds are key components in the choosing of a mate. Between those factors we can mention race, ethnic groups, religion, occupation, and education.

These similarities directly affect the choosing of a mate because it is the social group in which one generally moves, it is the group of young people with which you spend most of your time. It is the direct contact with this group of people where someone finally emerges as a possible candidate.

It has been demonstrated that similarities in personal characteristics as well as in common interests are of great importance when one is choosing a partner. This includes hobbies, height, weight, religious and political beliefs, physical appearance, to name just a few. People with high self-esteem look for people with high self-esteem, and those with low self-esteem look for those that also have low self-esteem, and so on.

The general idea in this area consists of how many similarities exist within a couple. Of course, there will be fewer differences and therefore a higher probability that they will get along well in marriage. It is no wonder that we are told that "those who are alike are mutually attracted, and those that are alike appreciate themselves" (Ellen G. White, *Patriarchs and Prophets*, page 174).

Young people tend to get married to the people with whom they are closest, that is to say, those who they see most frequently and with whom they spend the most time, like those from church, their neighborhood, their school, also with those that are of the same social class.

Others, however, are attracted by people that are opposite to them in certain areas. We have the case of some introverts that feel attracted by extroverted people and the majority of women prefer men that are taller than them.

There are some characteristics that people prefer to be different while there are others that they prefer to be the same. This, of course, varies between people and with each case. What is important, I will repeat, is to be alert to what the differences and the similarities are and the effect that they will have on the marriage relationship. If they are given serious consideration during the courtship and you reach a happy understanding, the possibilities are reduced that could cause problems during marriage.

The Filter

In the process of choosing a partner, all of the possible candidates go through a filter at different levels. This theory, suggested by the researchers Kerckhoff and Davis, presents a filter that has, at the same time, three other filters or parts: the endogamic filer, the homogamic filter, and the filter of complementary needs.

When selecting a partner, there is a big field of possible candidates for marriage, and from among all of them, several go through the first filter, the endogamic, because they have similar backgrounds: they go to the same school, the same church, live in the same neighborhood. You begin as friends and then go on to become "very good friends" or "special friends."

The second filter is narrower and more selective because only those with similar interests and characteristics go through this filter. Courtship helps us find those who are compatible with the desired interests and characteristics.

The third filter is narrower still. It is possible that several people go through the first two filters but the only people that go through the third filter are those that satisfy the most compelling needs. It is with these that one can get into a serious dating and sometimes become engaged to, which generally ends with a wedding.

Another very similar theory to the filter theory is the one that considers three aspects in the process of choosing a partner: stimulation, values, and roles.

This theory perceives the choosing of a partner as a market in which individuals try to obtain the best that they can, considering what they have to offer. In the stimulation process we see that the more similarities that exist between the different stimulating factors, the more possibilities there are that the two people will feel attracted to each other. Among those factors we can mention physical attraction, social competition, and economic situation. From this process some people go on to the area of values where a series of tests are carried out to discover the compatibility of their beliefs and values. Those that go through this process successfully enter into the third step that consists of a serious evaluation as to whether their expectations of what a spouse is will be satisfied or not by the candidate under consideration.

Courtships that successfully go through the three "filters" have high possibilities of culminating in marriage. Many, however, throw themselves into marriage after going through only one or two of the filters, considerably increasing the possibilities of ending in divorce.

Perhaps one of the most elaborate theories is the one that is presented by Robert Lewis, in which the dating relationship is developed through six stages, in each of which the seriousness of the relationship is increased. The stages are as follows:

1.   The perception of a person in the similarities that they believe they find in the other person, such as values, general interests, and personality traits.
2.   Establishment in the relationship of a certain degree of affinity that is evident due to good communication between them, positive evaluations of both, and general satisfaction in the relationship.
3.   Attraction to a higher intimacy due to the fact that they are open with each other.
4.   A clear perception and anticipation of the role that each one will play as a spouse in the marriage relationship.
5.   A clear adjustment that the role that they are to play fits into the needs of the future spouse.
6.   The serious crystallization of the relationship due to the progressive commitment of the couple, the establishment of limits, serious commitment, and the growing identity of the individuals as a couple.

All of the points in the different theories mentioned beforehand have a serious place in what is considered as the selection process of the partner and in certain cases they are applied more than in others. What I consider of high importance is that these theories can serve as reference points so that the couple can determine if the path that their courtship relationship is following is normal and of benefit or not.

The Triangle Theory

Authors Jack and Judy Balswick have a very interesting theory, especially for Christian young people, dealing with the most important factors that come into play in the choosing of a partner. The three elements are the influence that are exercised by the church or Christian community, the parents, and the young person that is searching for his or her partner.

Ideally, the influence of the three elements should be equal, that is to say, they should exercise the same influence. Therefore, the likes and wishes of the young person should be considered because they are the ones that are the most directly involved and affected; but the direction of the church or Christian community should also be attended to, and in the same manner the instruction and advice of the parents should be heard.

Not only do the parents and family have a high interest in the well-being of the couple, but so does the religious community, because directly and indirectly they are affected by what happens to the couple and therefore they need to be accounted for in the choosing of the partner and the formation of a new home.

In certain cultures and for certain young people, however, an equilateral triangle is not what is considered best, because in certain places the church or the Christian community is the one that predominantly decides. In other situations it is the parents that determine the choice of the partner, as in the case of arranged marriages. And in other situations it is the young person that decides with whom they are to form a home.

These influences or elements that affect the choice of a partner are represented by triangles where is presented to us, first of all, the biblical model or ideal where the three influences are considered equal (the equilateral triangle). The other triangles are not proportional, because they show a major emphasis, and at times it is unbalanced, whether it is in the Christian community, in the family, or in the individual.

Seeing that the personal element is predominant in our midst, that is to say, the decision lies mainly with the young person, it is important to stress the importance of considering the opinion and advice of other people, particularly those from the parents and from the Christian community. The following advice is very appropriate:

> "One of the greatest errors connected with this subject is that the young and inexperienced must not have their affections disturbed, that there must be no interference in their love experience. If there was a subject that needed to be viewed from every standpoint, it is this. The aid of the experience of others and a calm, careful weighing of the matter on both sides are positively essential. It is a subject that is treated altogether too lightly by the great majority of people. Take God and your God-fearing parents into your counsel, young friends. Pray over the matter" Ellen G. White (*The Adventist Home*, 73).

Chapter 7

Factors That Make For Success Or Failure

There is much sense in the saying that a marriage is not born but rather made. Marital happiness is the direct result of what has been invested in the relationship. A good marriage requires much attention and care so that it can come to be the blessing that it is intended to be. But how am I to know if my marriage will go well? Is there something that can give me an idea if I am headed in the right direction? What factors can navigate me towards the correct destination?

Although we cannot predict with complete certainty what will happen in a marriage, we can, however, have an idea or anticipate what the situation will be; we can see if a marriage is headed towards success or failure. There are certain factors whose presence or absence influence or determine to a great extent the happiness in marriage. These determinants are not final nor does it mean that there are no exceptions, but the couple needs to take them seriously into account so that they do not affect the happiness in your home.

Study after study has constantly demonstrated that the following factors weigh heavily in predicting the marital happiness of every couple. Serious consideration should be given to each one of them, especially for people that are planning to get married. The most important factors are the ones that are presented by researchers Carter and McGoldrick, in their work *The Family Life Cycle*.

Getting Married After a Loss

Whenever a couple gets married after a significant loss what they are trying to do is compensate for the loss. When someone gets married to recover the loss of some other relationship, whether it is marital or an engagement, the possibilities of unhappiness in the new relationship are very high.

This is due, without doubt, to the fact that the principal motive that took the person to marriage was not love or interest in the new relationship but rather to compensate for the loss. And it is not that there is something wrong in attempting to compensate for the lost relationship to fill the void that has been formed, but it is of great importance to focus and put into correct perspective the new relationship, recognizing that the new boyfriend or wife is not the person in the past relationship. And overall, you have to avoid comparisons which can be very painful and cause much harm to the new relationship.

Every person that has lost a significant relationship should give themselves the appropriate and necessary time before going into another serious relationship. It is important to assure oneself that the strongest part of the grief has passed and that the majority of the pain has been left behind. Some people will take more time than others, of course, but it is important to wait for the opportune time. It is true that a new relationship can help to forget or to get over the relationship that has been lost, but it is very important, in any case, to go through the necessary grief for the relationship that has been lost in order to put it all in the past.

Getting Married to Distance Yourself From Family

There are youth that lead a miserable life – or believe this to be the case – in the bosom of their family and to get out of this unhappy relationship they decide to get married. The desire to distance themselves from their family is the principal reason that leads many to get married.

To get married only to get away from family members does not produce a good marriage, because the emphasis, as in the previous case, is not in the desire to establish a new relationship but rather in ending the old.

On the other hand, it is of great importance to fix whatever problem exists, principally with parents or family members, in order to establish a marriage where true happiness exists. Those that have serious problems with their parents and other family members will soon find themselves in the same situation with their marriage partner. Therefore, getting married to get away from parents or other family members is not a valid reason to get married.

Getting Married With Great Differences

This has to do with something that is called "homogeneity" in marriage. Several researchers such as Becker, Bumpass, Sweet, and Norton, have found that heterogeneous marriages tend to experience greater disillusionment than homogenous marriages. The thought that opposites "attract" is being substituted by the belief that says that they "attack." Although it is true that it is almost impossible to find someone with whom you are alike in everything, and therefore there will always be differences, there are, however, certain differences that determine matrimonial happiness; some however, can be irreconcilable, impossible to overcome, and yet there will be people that can confront them without much difficulty. What is important is finding out about those differences before marriage and to understand that they can be a problem in the future. Of course, there will be exceptions, but those exceptions are not so much the result of coincidence as from the understanding of the problem on the part of the partners and great comprehension and love so as to not be seriously affected by those differences.

The differences that can produce big problems for the couple happen when the background of the married couple is different in the following areas.

Religion

It is very interesting to note that several studies have demonstrated that religion is a very significant factor in the prediction of matrimonial satisfaction, and when a couple that gets married has religious differences it can predict that there will be marital instability.

It is worth mentioning that this includes Christians from different denominations who report a high ratio of divorces. Grunlan points out that although the phrase "do not be yoked together with unbelievers" (2 Corinthians 6:14) refers particularly to marriages of believers with unbelievers, it certainly has certain implications for marriages of different Christian faiths.

It should be mentioned that marriages where religion plays an important part tend to register a greater level of matrimonial happiness. Researchers Ross, Sawhill, and Teachman have found that very religious people tend to divorce and separate less.

Education

It has been found that generally the higher the level of education of a couple, the less the possibilities of divorce. That is to say, as education increases the percentages of divorce is lowered. Statistics indicate something interesting on this issue: there is evidence that there is a sharp change when a woman reaches much higher levels of education, because then it is easier to do away with a marriage relationship that is not all that pleasant.

The effects in marriages of big differences in this area have not been amply demonstrated, but when it is in direct relation to the age at the time of getting married, the occupation, and/or financial incomes, then its effects on matrimonial happiness are demonstrated. This factor by itself might not be a serious indicator for predicting happiness in a marriage, but because it is generally accompanied by other factors, such as those mentioned previously, it is, therefore, a factor that needs to be seriously considered.

Social Class

Generally speaking, the higher the social class the less the possibility of a divorce. This might not necessarily indicate greater happiness, but we can think that by different strengths or special pressures, this type of people tend to get divorced with less frequency, or at least they wait longer than the average before getting divorced.

It appears that the problem generally occurs when you get married to someone from a different social class. In these situations, research has revealed that there exists greater marital conflict and higher possibilities of divorce. This is where the idea stems that you should seek to get married to someone of approximately the same social class so as to help in marital stability.

Ethnic Group

It has also been found that interracial marriages or marriage among different ethnic groups brings marital dissatisfaction and a high percentage of divorce.

Age

Several studies have demonstrated that when there is a great difference in age between spouses the possibility of unhappiness in marriage is much greater.

It is gauged that the ideal should be that the man be several years older than the woman, although more than ten would be to go beyond what is more or less normal.

Sociologists Teachman, Plonko, and Scanzoni point out that the differences with greatest consequences are the marriages with religious differences (especially when one of the two is Catholic), marriages with a great difference in age (especially if the wife is older), and interracial marriages.

Great differences in the areas mentioned before are factors that determine unhappiness in marriage and every couple should be alert to these differences. Of course, the more of these differences that are present in a relationship, the higher the possibilities of dissatisfaction.

Getting Married With an Incompatible constellation

No, this characteristic has absolutely nothing to do with zodiac symbols. Personally, I do not believe that astrology has anything to do with the formation of a happy marriage.

The compatible or incompatible constellation between siblings is a very interesting observation that is made due to the characteristics that each person has in accordance to the birth order within the family and the compatibility when they get married to someone whose birth order is not compatible with their own.

This idea is derived from the observation that has been proposed by the author Toman, suggesting that the birth order of siblings, the difference of genders, and the family configuration have a great influence over the personality traits and social tendencies of children.

Due to several conscious or unconscious pressures or expectations by the family, principally of parents, there are certain characteristics that are forged upon children that are in agreement with the birth order. The expectations of and the way that first borns are treated is different than the expectations and treatment of younger siblings and this affects, to a certain degree, their personality.

First borns, for example, tend to be dominant and directive, while younger siblings tend to be more dependent and followers. What happens when two first born children get married? Of course, both will want to dominate the relationship. What happens when a first born son gets married to a younger born female? In this case there will not be problems as to who is going to direct the marriage. He will gladly take control and she will concede without protesting. This explains, to a certain extent, the reason for certain incompatibilities and differences in the marital relationship.

According to Stephens, single children's success in marriage is less and they need to work harder in order to have a good relationship with those that come from families where there are multiple siblings.

Although this theory is very logical, it is in a very general manner, and as with everything there will be some very notable exceptions. However, I believe that it is very important to take it into consideration and discuss it before getting married.

Getting Married and Living Very Close
or Very Far From Family

Those who get married and live very close or very far from families of origin tend to report levels of unhappiness in their marriages. It would appear that as far as parents are concerned, one should not live too far or too close.

The distance of parents and marital happiness generally presents a curved graph line, in which being too close to family or too far produces marital instability.

Whoever is not ready to live independently from their parents is not ready to get married, in which case the new couple should live far removed from the parents. But not too far, because if they live too far, they will have difficulties in visiting them and part of happiness generally consists in visiting parents and keeping in touch with them.

Getting Married and Depending on the Family

It has been found that marriages report high levels of unhappiness if they depend upon family in a physical, emotional, or financial manner. This is completely in agreement with the law of marriage that we find in Genesis 2:24 in relation to father and mother. The Word of God clearly indicates, "Man will leave his father and mother and be united to his wife, and they will become one flesh".

In order to completely unite oneself with a woman and become one flesh, it is very important to first leave parents and become completely independent from them. Whoever is not ready or willing to leave dad and mom is not ready to get married. Marriage is for those who have absolute independence from their parents.

Getting Married At the Wrong Age

It would appear that there is an appropriate age at which to get married and achieve maximum results. It has been found that the majority of couples that get married before they are 20 years old or after they are 30 present problems of unhappiness in their marital relationship.

There is evidence that clearly indicates that there is an appropriate age to get married and this falls between 20 and 30 years of age. Perhaps the reason that one should not get married before turning 20 years old is because of the level of maturity of a person, and after 30 perhaps because they have become accustomed to living alone and it is difficult for them to adjust to the demands of a companion. It is therefore estimated that the ideal age to get married is around 25 years of age.

Getting Married in a Hurry

This has to do with the time that a couple dedicates to getting to know each other during the period of dating. A hurried courtship is destined for failure.

It has been found that a good courtship should not last less than six months, nor should it be more than three years. If we combine this factor with the previous one, we can reach the conclusion that the age to have a serious courtship or engagement should never happen before 18 years of age.

Getting Married Without Family Approval

It has been proven that if family members or close friends do not attend the wedding, there are certain negative effects on the marital happiness of the couple. This is probably due to the fact that in these cases family members are not invited because there are bad relationships with them due to the fact that they might be opposed to the wedding, and if they are opposed to the wedding, then they are not invited.

When relationships with certain family members are not good, happiness in general is affected in a direct or indirect manner, and this is why it has an effect on marital happiness.

It appears that family approval plays an important part in spousal happiness, therefore everything should be done that is possible to clear up whatever doubt there might be on the issue and seek some form of general family happiness.

Getting Married Once Pregnant or Having Children During the First Year of Marriage

Because every marriage requires a considerable period of adjustment, the later a couple waits to have children, the better. Therefore, getting married while pregnant or having children during the first year of marriage could stop a couple from concentrating on their relationship. The premature arrival of a child could act against the happiness of the couple.

In most cases it is advised that a couple wait two to five years before having their first child.

Getting Married When There Are Bad Relationships With Other Members of the Family

If one of the partners has bad relationships with siblings or parents it has been estimated that it will be an important factor against marital happiness. Stephens has demonstrated that individuals that have conflicts with their parents tend to report bad matrimonial adjustment.

Marriages do not function in a vacuum. The new family system includes and is also affected in a direct or indirect manner by other relationships, such as that of family members. That is why there is much truth in the saying that one gets married to a family and not just one person.

A problem that is often repeated is that many times parents or family members tell the girlfriend negative things about the boyfriend and later the girlfriend tells her boyfriend. The couple ends up getting married and the boyfriend is left feeling resentful for his entire life of the parents or family members of his wife. The sooner these problems can be addressed and fixed, the better.

Getting Married When You Think You Had an Unhappy Childhood

If one of the spouses considers their childhood or adolescence unhappy, this will bring difficulties in the marital adjustments of that person, probably due to the narrow and direct relationship that exists between general happiness and life and marital happiness.

Whoever had an unhappy childhood due to abuse, negligence, or some other negative circumstance, tends to experience unhappiness in all of the aspects of life and that affects the marriage relationship.

Getting Married To Someone Whose Family Patterns Were Unstable

This has to do with the type of family from which one comes, particularly when the family patterns of the spouses were unstable. The new marital relationship is directly affected. We cannot deny the great influence that the family of origin has over individuals and this becomes much more evident in marriage. Whatever one has seen in their homes, the manner in which parents treated each other, the type of communication, the discipline, the entire family life, all of this provides a script or model that ends up repeating itself in new homes.

Authors indicate that when one of the spouses had an unstable home that ended in divorce, their marital adjustment is much more negative than for those who come from intact and stable homes. And it would appear that this affects men more than women.

In this chapter we have seen factors that have shown they have a direct effect on marital happiness. This is not to say that if some of them are present it will not be possible to attain happiness. It can be done, as long as the couple is conscious of the problems that these factors can cause and work together in a dedicated manner so that the possible negative consequences do not affect their relationship. On the other hand, some of these factors that are present can be minimized and for this psychotherapy can be very effective.

Every couple that wishes to guarantee a happy marriage for themselves will do all that is possible in order to avoid all of those factors that are negative and can undermine the happiness of their new home and will work united so that those factors or consequences that cannot be avoided will affect them as little as possible.

Chapter 8

Sex and Dating

One of the gravest problems that young people encounter during their courtship is physical contact or sexual liberty. Up to what point should they express their love and care through physical contact? How do they maintain a healthy sexuality during this period of such high hormonal activity?

Someone has said that while dating young people go through the most serious metamorphosis, many of them turn into "octopuses," with hundred of hands touching everything then can. The deal is that sexuality is a fire that should not be played with. Whoever gets burned has to pay the sad consequences later.

The tragic news that the Los Angeles superstar, Magic Johnson, had the virus that produces AIDS continues to get attention from the news agencies. Johnson, who has become a member of the presidential commission of AIDS and promoter of "safe sex", said in a recent interview that because the majority of young people lead a very active sex life they should take certain precautions if they desire to avoid serious problems that can affect them for the rest of their lives.

Can it be that the majority of young people lead a very active sex life? What are the problems that accompany such activity? The mother of Rosa María discovered this sad reality once when she was cleaning the living room of her home. When she was picking up some magazines, a note fell to the floor from her daughter that was written to a counselor from the magazine. The note said: "I am 12 years old and I have had intimate sexual relations with my boyfriend. Can I get pregnant?"

Rosa Maria's case is not an isolated one. Several studies have demonstrated that by 19 years of age 79 percent of men and 66 percent of women will have had sexual relations. Generally women have their first sexual experience when they are 16 years old and a man when he is 17.

Unfortunately, many begin very early in their lives. The Gutmacher Institute informs us that 4 percent begin at 12 yeas of age, representing more than 100,000 young people. The percentage increases with age: 10 percent at 13 years old; 20 percent at 14; 29 percent at 15; and 46 percent at 16 years of age. As a result, approximately half of all births outside of marriage and one-third of abortions are adolescent mothers. At this pace, four of every 10 girls will experience being pregnant at least once during their adolescence, seeing that more than 12 million adolescents are sexually active in the United States.

The decision to have a sexually active life produces a sequence of events in young people where decisions of great importance must be made that will seriously affect their lives. Dr. Brent C. Miller has treated many cases of sexually active young people and has found a series of complex alternatives among which young people have to decide. If the decision is to lead an active sexual life, they must decide to use contraceptives. Because more than half of the young people do not use any form of contraceptives, pregnancy is the result. The next important decision has to do with whether to keep the child or if it will be aborted. If it is not aborted, then follows the decision to keep the child or give it up for adoption. Only 4 percent decides to give their child up for adoption; from the 96 per cent that keep the child, less than half get married, and therefore a big percentage of these young girls become single moms. Each of these decisions, primarily the last ones, produce an elevated dose of anxiety and stress due to the consequences and effects that are produced in the life of every young person. However, pregnancy is not the only problem or risks that result from the promiscuous attitude that young people have towards sex in general. A premature and irresponsible sexual life carries the high risk of contracting venereal diseases, such as AIDS, herpes, or some other illness that can result in chronic infections where the least result can be infertility.

The magazines *American Public Health* and *Wall Street* present recent studies that tell us that among young girls ages 12 to 15 who have had sexual experiences, the tendency toward suicide is six times greater that among those who are virgins. Among mothers that have not graduated from high school, the tendency to kill their babies is three times greater. Girls express more feelings of doubt, loss of self esteem, uncertainty, anxiety, loneliness, and lack of help. Boys experience a high sense of guilt, stress, and heavy responsibility. The most dramatic psychiatric results are the tendency towards suicide and to psychosis after the birth of the baby. Due to the opportunity to remain in school girls that have not had children outside of marriage tend to have a social and economic life which is much more stable.

On the other hand, a series of researchers such as Trussell, Ruo, DeMaris, Leslie and Watson tell us, in publications such as the *Journal of Marriage and the Family* and *Family Relations*, that the young people that have avoided serious problems by making the correct decision at the beginning, that is to say, the decision of not having an active sexual life, reach greater happiness and security in their marriages.

Why is it that some young people decide, despite the great risks, to carry on an active sexual life while others prefer abstinence? What factors contribute to making this decision? Sexual conduct is tremendously influenced by a complex series of psychological and sociological factors. Among the most important factors that determine the sexual conduct among young people we can mention the following:

Social Influence

Our society definitely models our sexual knowledge and attitude, especially during our childhood and adolescence. Young people today have grown up and are maturing in a very permissive culture that is charged with sexual stimulation. Almost all of the studies that examine the sources of sexual information, such as those carried out by Strouse and Fabes, published in *Adolescence*, demonstrate that the pressure of the group is of greatest importance, followed by the influence of television.

For many young people to have a boyfriend or girlfriend is vital for their self esteem. And many young girls feel that having sexual relations is a price that they have to pay for it. Laura was a victim of this pressure when she was 15 years old. "All of my female friends spoke as if they knew everything about sex. I felt bad because I was the only virgin in the group." Boys use sexuality to win the favor of their companions. Marcos tells us, "The attitude between my classmates is that if you are not sexually involved you are a retarded dumb person." To win acceptance and popularity among his classmates Marcos and Laura became a couple and in a few weeks they began their sexual relationship.

With the continuous increase of sexual messages on television, young people are constantly bombarded with erotic messages. Soap operas, which attract a great number of young people, are saturated with sexual messages; of the sexual expressions that are presented, 49 percent happen among lovers, 29 percent among strangers, and only 6 percent happens among married couples. Among "prime time" programs (schedules with the greatest number of television viewers), 89 percent of sexual scenes happen outside of marriage, according to studies that have been carried out by Strouse and Fabes. There is no escape even during commercials, because the majority of products are sold using sexual connotations.

Lack of Sexual Education

Several authors agree that sexual promiscuity among young people is due to the lack of education in this area. And since only 10 percent of young people have received appropriate sexual education, Peter Scales concludes that it is obvious to see the problem associated with sexuality among young people in a period of so little sexual education.

Some people fear that the sexual education of their children will prepare them to have premature sexual experiences; that it is like giving them a class on how to steal. However, several surveys indicate that young people that take sexual education classes do not become more liberal in their attitudes. On the contrary, according to the surveys of Casey and Peterson reported in *Children Today,* when parents sexually educate their children they follow a more traditional path in their sexual conduct and young women in their college years tend not to have sexual relations when their mother is the greatest source of sexual information.

Lack of Moral and Religious Values

The magazine *Sexuality Today* informs us that recent studies have also revealed that the following factors reduce the incidences of sexual activities between young people: Attending church one or more times a week, if the mother has 12 or more years of education, if the parents have not been divorced, and if they have had sexual education.

The grave problem is that not only young people, but also their parents are confused about the diverse sexual and moral values that exist today and they are unsure about what they wish to communicate to their children. The transmission of high moral values to the children requires a highly charged dose of good examples by way of the parents. It is the lack of firm moral principles in the home that has produced the present generation of sexually promiscuous and liberal young people.

A Correct Attitude Toward Sex

What is a correct attitude toward sex? What are the orientating principles and moral guides that should be followed in order to lead a responsible sexual life?

Jack and Judy Balswick correctly point out that today in our society there are four philosophies in regard to the sexual conduct of young people: sexual abstinence, the double standard, sexuality when there is affection, and sexuality even if there is no affection.

Sexual abstinence continues to be the traditional Christian standard and, although it is one of the most firm positions, it is refused by the majority of the members of our society.

The double standard that allows sexual activity for men but not for women. This philosophy has declined in the last 60 years, due to the fact that women feel that they also should be an active part in the deal and that society allows it.

Sexuality when there is affection is the philosophy that is most accepted in actuality. If both people appreciate themselves, even if there is not any type of commitment between them, or even if they are married or engaged to other people, this is enough of a reason to have sexual relations.

Sexuality even if there is no affection is the one that proposes casual and recreational sex between two people in mutual agreement. This last position grew the most in popularity in the last 20 years but has lost strength recently due to contemporary venereal diseases. The risks involved have led many ex-promiscuous people to say, "I like sex but I am not willing to die for it."

In order to appropriate a correct philosophy about sex, it is important to remember that sex is a very important aspect of each living being and especially of human beings. The sexual desires and reactions are natural parts of our body; they are intrinsic components of our personality. It is a method of procreation and continuity created by God for our human existence. Sex is not only the sole method of procreation, but rather it is an important manner in which to demonstrate intimacy and affection between two people in love. It is the knowledge of the body of the other person and, different from animals, it provides the entrance into the world of their emotions; it is therefore the closest relationship that two people can experience. It is the manner in which two people be one. It is not about a game or a casual union, but rather it involves a high sense of commitment and responsibility, because the people are left psychologically united forever. It is because of this that the most favorable context for sexuality is in the marriage relationship. There is no "safe sex" before or outside of marriage. It is in the marriage relationship where you can and should give the most sublime expression of love through sexuality.

Principles of Sexuality

Dr. Smedes, in his classic work *Sex for Christians* presents three important principles about sexuality: sexuality is an integral part of our being, we are sexual beings because we were created this way by our God; sexuality is the medium of expression of the most intimate relationship between two people; it is a union of heterosexual character inside of the context of a commitment of love.

According to these important principles, we are sexual beings, sex is an intrinsic component of our being, and it is the expression of greatest intimacy that two human beings can experience. But this very important aspect of our life and one with such serious consequences should be used in a responsible manner and should be reserved for expression inside of the marital relationship, because marriage produces the atmosphere in which the most intimate manifestations of love and kindness can be carried out. It is for this reason that the law of God condemns premarital, extramarital, and homosexual sexual relations (1 Cor 6:9, 18; Exo 20:14; Lev 18:22; 1 Tim 1:10).

How Far Should Couples Go?

But since it is also natural for single people, particularly couples, to express affection in a physical manner, how far, then, can couples go in demonstrating intimacy and affection in their relationships? Considering that the lack of physical contact as well as too much of the same can be negative in human relationships, what should be the middle ground between young people who are dating? How far can a couple go?

The crisis or critical point in physical contact between couples is produced when there is sexual excitement. Because the culmination of sexual excitement is orgasm, the farther one advances in excitement the closer one comes to orgasm.

Generally speaking, physical or sexual advancements that culminate in orgasm are carried out through the following steps:

Hand to hand

The first contact that happens between couples is almost always visual. The physical presence of the other person is discovered through visual contact. And when there is an interest, they fix it so that the next step happens, verbal contact. But the first physical contact between couples is almost always that of touching and holding each others hands, which produces an extraordinary sensation, because it is the "biggest sign" that they are a couple. Whoever sees two young people holding hands knows immediately that they are a couple. To take this important step without understanding some form of commitment can bring about some serious frustrations and emotional conflicts.

Hand to body

Holding someone's hand is generally followed by a hug, holding each other around the waist (hips), caressing the other's hair and arms. To be allowed to hold another persons hand almost serves as an "authorization" so that other parts of the body can be touched.

Mouth to mouth

In the physical contact between people in love, there is no experience that is more exciting and that can bring about such ecstasy as the kiss. This is one of the most extraordinary experiences; the first kiss, the second, and the third, and all of the ones that follow. A kiss can be, and is, an experience that is charged with emotions and although there are different types of kisses, this is a very intimate experience for couples.

Hand to breasts

Generally a kiss is accompanied by hugs and the hand moves surreptitiously over the body. This is where many become "octopuses." There are hands that come out of everywhere! If the excitement is too great and unmeasured in the kiss, it can be perceived as an invitation or permission that can carry a young man to advance until he touches her breasts, something that can be extremely stimulating and exciting and that can become the point of no return for many. This step should be completely outside of the physical contact realm that Christian young people should experience.

This is where Pastor Wilkerson in his book, *Straight Answers*, suggests that young women could be of great help to young men by not allowing them to advance more than they should. On those occasions, we are told, they should remember Ecclesiastes 9:10 "Whatever your hand finds to do, do *it* with *all* your might." Wilkerson says: "Lift up your hand and in the name of the Lord, smack him hard on the mouth."

Mouth to breasts

Whoever gives way in the previous step finds it very difficult to control themselves in order not to go any further and the hand grabbing is guided by the uncontrollable passion that is advancing more in its excitement that finds its satisfaction in orgasm.

Hand to genitals

After the mouth and the hand have touched and excited some very stimulating parts of the body, the next target is to advance to the center of sexual activities: the genitals and sexual organs.

Genitals to genitals

Generally the hand arrives first, followed at times by the mouth and finally by the genitals, consummating in this way the sexual act, that in the case of young couples is known as the sin of fornication. The words of Dr. Peñalosa are very opportune when we are told that it is almost impossible for the boyfriend to maintain his respect and for the girlfriend to keep her respect when both have been accomplices in the shadows. Each time a boyfriend invites his girlfriend to the kingdom of darkness and she accepts, relationships are produced that are less dignified and more compelling. They return with their souls full of shadows. It also becomes nighttime in their hearts. And the truth is that passion nests itself in the darkness, while love lives in the sun and the outdoors.

Some people ask, "Why should I wait until I am married? Why not taste before to know if there will be a sexual compatibility between the couple?" These questions are good but are based on a false premise because, apart from the fact that fornication is a sin, what if you later decide not to get married? Besides, several studies such as those of Trussell and Ruo, DeMaris and Leslie, and Watson (cited in *Journal of Marriage and the Family*, 1984 and 1989; and *Family Relations*, 1983), have clearly indicated that whoever is involved in premarital sexual relationships or whoever cohabitates before getting married, tends to experience less matrimonial satisfaction.

About the argument that some people present that it is important for one of the two, especially the man, to have experience before getting married, the writer Carlos Cuauhtémoc Sánchez, in his "best seller" *Juventud en éxtasis* (Young people in ecstasy) illustrates it in the following way:

> To experiment sex for the first time is like going to Disneyland for the first time: everything is fascinating, you enjoy everything intensely, everything is a cause for investigating and enthusiasm; if you do it with someone that you love, the emotions that are lived will go without any trash, they will be genuine, for the two of you, do you understand me? On the other hand, if you have gone to Disneyland thirty times, accompanied by thirty different people and finally you go with the girl of your dreams, the succession will be very different: you will tell her what ride to get on, what line to form in and what she should look at; your advantage might help her in a certain respect and it will make you look superior, but as a couple, you will not feel any complicity or mutual trust; people are united in true love only when they learn together, when they share transcendent events for both and not when one demonstrates to the other their experience (p. 44).

Once the sexual act has been experienced as a couple, it is difficult to revert to any of the previous steps. Once it has been tasted a person will not be satisfied with just holding hands or kissing, they want it all. But even those that have advanced to the end can make serious resolutions to help themselves mutually so they do not do it again. This will be a great benefit and advantage for both.

Some Principles

It is important to decide at the beginning of a relationship what it is that one wants in that relationship, if it is appropriate, and how far they will go in their relationship. To help in these decisions, Jack and Judy Balswick present the following principles:

1.   The degree of sexual intimacy of couples should correspond to the degree of love and commitment in the relationship. If there is no love or commitment, intimacy is inappropriate because the focus is on the physical and not in the relationship. When there is love and commitment, being with the other person is more important than the pleasure that comes from physical intimacy.

2.   There is a physics law that tells us that in order to achieve the same effect twice, a stronger force must be applied. This law can be applied not only to the physical, but also to the sexual. The first kiss, for example, produces an extraordinary experience. However, as time goes by the effect of the kiss diminishes and the tendency is to increase the physical intensity in order to achieve the same stimulation. The ultimate sexual expression is orgasm. The more one advances in this direction the more difficult it becomes to return to the previous level. It is important to have this in mind and not advance too much attempting to determine with anticipation the appropriate limits for physical contact.

3.   What motivates physical contact? Is it to demonstrate affection or to sexually excite one another? If the objective is to gratify the ego instead of achieving a better personal relationship, then you are dealing with a selfish satisfaction.

4. It is important that there be a continual communication about every area of a relationship that exists between two people: social, psychological, emotional, and spiritual. When the physical dimension is developed out of proportion, the relationship in general becomes weak and vulnerable.

5. Both should assume the responsibility of establishing the direction of their relationship and to place limits on their physical relationship. Christian young people should reject the liberal idea that men should advance as far as they can in terms of sexuality and that it is the woman's responsibility to establish the limits. Both are equally responsible.

6. Couples should reach an agreement in relation to the limits that are proposed by their companion with the norms of conduct that are most conservative. This attitude of respect and love places a person above sexual desires. In the end, honoring the limitations demonstrates that one's companion is highly valued and appreciated, bringing the relationship to a high level of emotional intimacy. All of this eliminates the possibility that in the heat of passion these young people will carry out acts which they will later regret.

Whoever guides themselves by high moral and spiritual principles and knows what is to their best interest, avoids many difficulties as they make the correct decision at the very beginning of their life, of not activating themselves sexually until the moment that, together with their beloved, they make a commitment, before God and society, of being each others companions – the one for the other.

Premarital Inventory

I. Personal Information

1. Name _____

2. Address _____

3. Date _____

4. Gender _____

5. Age _____

6. Telephone _____

7. Name of Significant Other _____

8. Nationality _____

9. Race _____

10. Citizenship _____

11. Occupation _____

12. Highest level of education reached _____

13. Studies in progress _____

14. Date of graduation _____

15. Number of brothers _____

16. Number of sisters _____

17. Marital status of parents
    - ☐ Married
    - ☐ Divorced
    - ☐ Separated
    - ☐ Separated by death
    - ☐ Multiple marriages

18. Type of community that your childhood and youth were spent in
    - ☐ Rural
    - ☐ Town

☐ Small City
☐ Big City

19. Economic status of parents in the community:
☐ Poor
☐ Middle class
☐ Rich

20. Greatest problem during your childhood or youth:_____

21. Generally you consider that your childhood was:
☐ Very happy
☐ Happy
☐ Somewhat happy
☐ Somewhat unhappy
☐ Unhappy
☐ Very unhappy

22. You consider that the bond between your father and you is:
☐ Strong
☐ Considerable
☐ Regular
☐ Hostile
☐ Considerably hostile
☐ Very hostile

23. The bond with your mom is:
☐ Strong
☐ Considerable
☐ Regular
☐ Hostile
☐ Considerably hostile
☐ Very hostile

24. Your level of independence from your parents:
☐ Very adequate
☐ Good
☐ Inadequate

25. You wish that your father was more:

_____

_____

_____

26. You wish that your mother was more:

_____

_____

_____

27. You consider that your parents type of discipline was:
    - ☐ Very severe
    - ☐ Severe
    - ☐ Moderate
    - ☐ Regular (appropriate)
    - ☐ There was no discipline
    - ☐ Inconsistent

28. You consider that the marital adjustment between your parents was:
    - ☐ Very happy
    - ☐ Happy
    - ☐ Somewhat happy
    - ☐ Somewhat unhappy
    - ☐ Unhappy
    - ☐ Very unhappy

29. Number of previous serious commitments_____

30. What there a problem with alcoholism or substance abuse in your immediate family?   ☐ Yes   ☐ No

31. Was there a problem of physical abuse in your family?
                                                ☐ Yes   ☐ No

32. Have you been married before?   ☐Yes   ☐No

II.   Information about the couple

33. How long have you known each other? _____
34. How long have you been dating? _____
35. Date of engagement _____
36. Probable date of marriage _____

37. Things that I most like about my boyfriend/ girlfriend?

_____
_____
_____
_____
_____
_____

38. Things that I don't like about my boyfriend/ girlfriend?

_____
_____
_____
_____
_____
_____

III.   **Communication**

39. Do you have many problems in your relationship?
    ☐ Yes ☐ No

40. When you talk, you generally spend time talking about:

_____
_____
_____
_____
_____

41. You need to talk more about

_____
_____
_____
_____
_____

42. Your greatest communication problem is:

_____
_____
_____

43. Do you believe that you need to be understood better?
   ☐ Yes   ☐ No

44. It is very difficult for you to speak when:

_____

_____

_____

_____

_____

45. Do you find it difficult to express your emotions?
   ☐ Yes   ☐ No

46. Do you prefer to evade problems rather than confront them?   ☐ Yes   ☐ No

47. Do you think that you are at fault when there is a problem?
   ☐ Yes   ☐ No

48. Do you feel that there are issues in your relationship that you are not in agreement over? If so, what are they?

_____

_____

_____

_____

49. When you discuss a problem with your boyfriend/girlfriend you speak:
   ☐ With great difficulty
   ☐ Easily
   ☐ With difficulty
   ☐ Very easily

50. When there is a conflict in your relationship, what method do you utilize in order to resolve it?
   ☐ The girlfriend gives in
   ☐ The boyfriend gives in
   ☐ The conflict is not resolved
   ☐ It is resolved through compromise
   ☐ Some items are avoided, which cause unhappiness

51. Average time that is spent together, during a week _____

52. Time in a week that you dedicate to constructive conversation_____

IV. Finances

53. Have you adequately discussed your financial plans?
    ☐ Yes   ☐ No

54. Who managed the finances in your home? _____

55. Will you depend on financial help from any of your parents?   ☐ Yes   ☐ No

56. Where will you live when you get married? _____

57. Have you discussed the following topics?

Family Budget	☐ Yes	☐ No
Savings and investments	☐ Yes	☐ No
Checking account	☐ Yes	☐ No
Who will manage the money?	☐ Yes	☐ No
Who will pay the bills?	☐ Yes	☐ No
Wife working outside	☐ Yes	☐ No
Credit Cards	☐ Yes	☐ No
Tithes and Offerings	☐ Yes	☐ No
Buying of a house	☐ Yes	☐ No
Limits on debts	☐ Yes	☐ No

Monthly Budget

Prepare a monthly budget as detailed as possible:

Income:

_____ $ _____
_____ $ _____
_____ $ _____
_____ $ _____

Total Income $ _____

Expenses:

_____ $ _____

_____	$ _____
_____	$ _____
_____	$ _____
_____	$ _____
_____	$ _____
_____	$ _____
_____	$ _____
Total Expenses	$ _____
Total Income	$ _____
Total Expenses	$ _____
Grand Total	$ _____

V. Sexuality

58. Have you discussed the level of physical intimacy that you will permit prior to getting married?
☐ Yes   ☐ No

59. Have you spoken about premarital sexual relations?
☐ Yes   ☐ No

60. Have you spoken about sexual practices in your marriage?
☐ Yes   ☐ No

61. Have you spoken about birth control?
☐ Yes   ☐ No

62. How free have you been in demonstrated physical affection?
☐ Very inhibited
☐ Inhibited
☐ Somewhat inhibited
☐ Somewhat free
☐ Very free
☐ Uncontrollable

63. How important is sexuality in marriage?
☐ Not extremely important
☐ Somewhat important

☐ Important
☐ Very important
☐ Extremely important

64. Where do you plan to spend your honeymoon? _____

65. Have you spoken about your general plans for your honeymoon?   ☐ Yes   ☐ No

66. Have you spoken about your first night together?
          ☐ Yes   ☐ No

67. What preoccupies you the most about sexuality is:

_____
_____
_____

68. Answer F (False) or T (True) for the following:
___Men know all about sex
___Women know all about sex
___Men should always take the initiative
___Women should always take the initiative
___Sex is the most important aspect of marriage
___Premarital sex does not affect marriage
___Extramarital sex does not affect marriage
___Orgasm for the wife is of great importance
___In marital sexuality, everything is fair
      (everything is allowed)

VI.   Children

69. Do you plan to have children?   ☐ Yes   ☐ No
70. What do you think about adopting a child? _____
71. Have you discussed discipline for children? ☐ Yes☐ No
72. When do you plan to have your first child? _____
73. How many children do you plan to have? _____

VII.   In-laws and Family

74. What is the relationship of your girlfriend/ boyfriend with your parents? _____

_____

75. How do you get along with your parent-in-laws?
    _____
    _____
    _____

76. How do you get along with the siblings of your boyfriend/girlfriend? _____
    _____
    _____

77. Have you discussed how you are going to relate to your families in the future?   Yes   ☐ No

78. Do either of you emotionally depend on your parents?
    ☐ Yes   ☐ No

79. How frequently do you plan to visit your families? _____

80. Do your parents agree with your courtship?
    ☐ Yes   ☐ No

81. Do your parents agree with your marriage?
    ☐ Yes   ☐ No

82. Do your parents-in-law agree with your courtship?
    ☐ Yes   ☐ No

83. Do your parents-in-law agree with your marriage?
    ☐ Yes   ☐ No

VIII.   Religion

84. Denomination that you were born in or that you were raised in when a child or youth _____

85. Denomination that you belong to today _____

86. Do you believe that you have adequately discussed what you plan to do in regards to religion in your marriage?
    ☐ Yes   ☐ No

87. Have you discussed the following?

    – Religious education of the children
      ☐ Yes   ☐ No

– Time for family devotion
      ☐ Yes   ☐ No

- Observing the day of rest
      ☐ Yes   ☐ No

– Attending church
      ☐ Yes   ☐ No

– Participation in activities at church
      ☐ Yes   ☐ No

– Prayer before meals
      ☐ Yes   ☐ No

– Prayer together before bedtime
      ☐ Yes   ☐ No

– Personal devotions
      ☐ Yes   ☐ No

– Religious ideas
      ☐ Yes   ☐ No

– Expectations from family members
      ☐ Yes   ☐ No

88. What is your interest in religious affairs?
    1   2   3   4
    Low interest   Much interest

89. What is the interest of your boy-/girl-friend toward religious affairs?
    1   2   3   4
      Low interest   Much interest

IX.   **Activities and Recreation**

90. What activities do you participate in that your boy-/girl-friend does not?

    _____

    _____

    _____

91. What activities does your boy-/girl-friend participate in that you do not?

    _____

    _____

    _____

92. What activities do you both participate in?

_____

_____

_____

93. What activities would you like it if you both participated in?

_____

_____

_____

94. Do you have any conflict in relation to your activities and recreation? ☐ Yes   ☐ No
If yes, explain: _____

_____

_____

X.   Marriage

95. List the things that preoccupy you and that cause you problems in relation to your future marriage:

_____

_____

_____

96. Describe your married life five years after getting married:

_____

_____

_____

97. If you separate or get divorced, it will be because:

_____

_____

_____

98. Circle the number that best indicates how ready you are to get married:
1   2   3   4   5   6   7   8   9   10
Not prepared   Very prepared

99. Circle the number that best indicates how emotional you are to get married:

       1   2   3   4   5   6   7   8   9   10

      Not emotional   Very emotional

100. Circle the number that best indicates the desire that you have to get married:

       1   2   3   4   5   6   7   8   9   10

      No desire   Desire very much

101. Things that would impede your wedding:

_____

_____

_____

102. For what reasons could your wedding be postponed?

_____

_____

_____

_____

103. Have you discussed the following details about the wedding?

– Church or location	☐ Yes	☐ No
– Minister or person to officiate	☐ Yes	☐ No
– Wedding attendants	☐ Yes	☐ No
– Invitations	☐ Yes	☐ No
– Reception	☐ Yes	☐ No
– Church decoration	☐ Yes	☐ No
– Decoration of reception hall	☐ Yes	☐ No
– Wedding coordinator(s)	☐ Yes	☐ No
– Photographer	☐ Yes	☐ No
– Video	☐ Yes	☐ No
– Wedding Cake	☐ Yes	☐ No
– Food	☐ Yes	☐ No
– Transportation	☐ Yes	☐ No

104. Your marriage will be successful if your boy-/girl-friend makes the following changes:

_____

_____

105. Your marriage will be happy if you make the following changes:

_____

_____

_____

_____

106. Write the marriage vows that you would like to use in your wedding:

_____

_____

_____

_____

_____

_____

_____

_____

_____

_____

_____

_____

_____

_____

_____

_____

_____

_____

_____

_____

_____

_____

_____

_____

_____

_____

Chapter 10

For Happy Marriages, Happy Dating

In the previous chapter more than 100 questions were provided on different subjects that should be discussed by every couple before taking the important step of marriage. The general idea is to provide the most important subjects that every couple should consider and discuss very seriously. It is of much value to do this before and not after marriage.

Although every couple can carry out a serious consideration of each and every point, the professional intervention of a counselor can be of great benefit to help them see things as objectively as possible and to indicate some of the points that should be dealt with more seriously or with greater fullness. This will help so that the adjustment of dating and later of marriage can be carried out harmoniously and therefore a happy marriage can be attained.

In this process, however, many couples will find out that their courtship lacks the necessary elements for the formation of a happy marriage. In these cases, it is much better not to proceed with the relationship. Although breaking a relationship that is as important as a dating or engagement, produces traumatic situations, these are preferable to continuing towards a marriage that does not have any hope of survival. It is of great importance to not ignore, during dating, those manifestations of character with which one of the two is not in agreement. It is very important to discuss them thoroughly and make serious decisions on the issue. Unfortunately many couples ignore these manifestations during the dating period and later the couple complains bitterly during marriage.

One should always have in mind that dating is there for the purpose of getting to know the other person and to know if the happy marriage that is desired can be achieved with them. And to know a person it is necessary to connect with them for a reasonable period of time. It is true that one will never get to know the other person completely while dating, because during marriage people continues to get to know each other, but it is vital to have the most amount of knowledge possible in regards to likes, desires, plans, values and ambitions of the other person to be able to know if they are compatible or not.

If several important elements are not present in the relationship, it is best to end it. The presence of love is basic, but love is not blind. True love is produced in a relationship where maturity and reason are predominant. As I write this paragraph I am strongly impressed with the idea that the world love forms an acrostic of great importance for every relationship of courtship.

Dating exists to get to know the other person and to discover if you can achieve that happy marriage that you are searching for with him or her. And to get to know a person it is necessary to spend a reasonable amount of time together. It is true that we can never get to another person completely during a courtship, because during a marriage we continue to get to know each other, but it is vital to have the greatest knowledge possible about the likes, desires, plans, values, and ambitions of the other person in order to discover whether or not you are compatible.

If several of the important elements are not present in your relationship, your best option is to terminate it. The presence of love is basic, but love is not blind. True love is produced in a relationship where maturity and reason predominate. As I write this paragraph, the idea that love can be used as something of great importance for every relationship of courtship has impressed me greatly.

The love of God

If we are not recipients of this love we cannot then love anyone in the whole sense of the word. We need to experience the love of God and project it after to the people that surround us, especially our boyfriend or girlfriend. The need to be and feel loved is something that is intrinsic to every human being. The love of God fills that emptiness that we all have and it enables us to genuinely love every one else.

It is important to assure ourselves that we possess this love and that our boyfriend or girlfriend also has this love that comes from our God in high esteem and that it is expressed in a genuine and sincere way.

Personal maturity

Dating is the preview to marriage. This is a very serious commitment and it should be considered thoroughly. If someone has not reached personal maturity, they are a poor judge in trying to make this decision that carries such transcendental consequences. This personal maturity can be seen in the attitudes and actions that a person demonstrates in the face of the decisions and difficulties that present themselves throughout life. We can heed the following warning:

"Boys and girls enter upon the marriage relation with unripe love, immature judgment, without noble, elevated feelings, and take upon themselves the marriage vows, wholly led by their boyish, girlish passions..." (Ellen G. White, *Messages for Young People*, 452).

All boyfriends and girlfriends should keep their eyes wide open observing the mature or immature attitude with which their mate responds in different circumstances.

Prayer

Getting married is an adventure in faith. One cannot be 100% certain as to how marriage will go for them. And just as our parents are very interested in our future, so is our Heavenly Father. And if we ask his guidance through prayer, we have all certainty that He will grant us His help. Prayer is the key in every courtship and marriage relationship.

"If men and women are in the habit of praying twice a day before they contemplate marriage, they should pray four times a day when such a step is anticipated. Marriage is something that will influence and affect your life, both in this world and in the world to come." (Ellen G. White, *The Adventist Home*, 71).

Couples should pray for each other so that God can guide their decisions. They should pray together and on their own in a personal way. During premarital counseling I always ask the couple to pray together each time that they visit and that every day, at a particular time, the pray for each other. I also suggest to them that they should ask their parents to pray for them every day so that God will clearly indicate the path that they should take. If "the family that prays together stays together," without a doubt the same can be said about a dating couple.

Reason and Respect

These two characteristics are too important to pass by. As mentioned before, love is not blind, reason is the foundation and respect is its most clear manifestation.

The couple that does not demonstrate respect to each other and does not guide itself by what reasoning indicates can have the certainty that it is not genuine love that unites them. the use of sanctified reasoning will help us make the most asserted decisions; and the different manifestations of respect will help us to cultivate and fortify the relationship.

Marriage is an art. And the participants not only need the instruments to develop this art but also the strong desire to do the best within their possibilities. Because of this it is necessary to listen to the advice of those around them, to dedicate sufficient time to the relationship, to read everything that is possible on the subject, to change those things that are considered harmful for the relationship and to constantly acquire all of those positive things that are needed to make of marriage a "true heaven upon this earth".

I finish with the following advice that sums up the essential characteristics that every young man and young woman should have before getting married:

"Under such guidance let a young woman accept as a life companion only one who possesses pure, manly traits of character, one who is diligent, aspiring, and honest, one who loves and fears God. Let a young man seek one to stand by his side who is fitted to bear her share of life's burdens, one whose influence will ennoble and refine him, and who will make him happy in her love." (Ellen G. White, *Messages for Young People*, 435-436).